MOMMY'S
LOCKED
in the
BATHROOM

MOMMY'S LOCKED

in the

BATHROOM

Surviving Your Child's
Early Years
with Your Sanity
and salvation
Intact!

CYNTHIA SUMNER

BARBOUR
PUBLISHING

© 2003 by Cynthia Sumner

The author is represented by Alive Communications, Inc., 7680 Goddard St., Suite 200, Colorado Springs, CO 80920.

ISBN 1-58660-979-3

All Scripture quotations are taken from the HOLY BIBLE: NEW INTERNATIONAL VERSION ®. NIV ®. Copyright © 1973, 1978, 1984 by the International Bible Society. Used by permission of Zondervan Publishing House. All rights reserved.

Published by Barbour Publishing, Inc., P.O. Box 719, Uhrichsville, Ohio 44683 www.barbourbooks.com

Our mission is to publish and distribute inspirational products offering exceptional value and biblical encouragement to the masses.

ecpa Member of the
Evangelical Christian
Publishers Association

Printed in the United States of America

5 4 3

To my children, Spencer, Shelby, and Ross,

who are the stars in my Orion's Belt.

Thank you for making me a mom.

Acknowledgments

A heartfelt thank you goes out to—

My husband, John—for supporting my every endeavor with love, and for getting dinner on the table so I could write.

My children, Spencer, Shelby, and Ross—for accepting less time spent together so I could realize my dream, and for all the great material.

My parents, Be and Van Wolford—for your excellent proofreading skills, and for being my own personal cheerleading squad.

The members of my book discussion group: Tina Acree, Deanna Lustfeldt, Anne Zumwalt, Kathy Orme, Cheryl Geiger, Barbie Becker, Liz Martin, and Joan Cook—for your willingness to share your hearts and memories, and for putting up with my quirky book selections.

My friends Lisa Gocken, Sally Allhands, Sherri Devine, and Dove Wong—for remaining my friends through thick and thin.

My friends at MOPS International, especially Beth Lagerborg, Beth Jusino, and Carol Kuykendall—for giving me the opportunity to find my voice and the means to make it heard.

My agent, Chip MacGregor—for your expert guidance, and for not giving up on me in spite of my overly busy schedule.

My editor, Shannon Hill—for your vision and direction, and for sharing your idea.

Contents

Introduction

Be shepherds of God's flock that is under your care...
not because you must, but because you are willing, as God wants you to be.

1 PETER 5:2

To say I was naive about the requirements of being a mom before having children of my own would be a huge under-statement. In fact, there are probably few new moms out there as woefully unprepared as I was for life with young children! Sure, I had the requisite baby-sitting jobs as a teenager, but during the fourteen years between baby-sitting part-time and becoming a mom, I spent little to no time around young children, and I avoided infants like the plague.

So there were many elements of motherhood that were a surprise: physically, emotionally, and spiritually. For example, in childbirth class I asked our teacher about the occasional sharp pain I was feeling in my groin area. "That's just your hips spreading," she replied. "Will they go back to normal?" I asked hopefully, being already well-endowed in the hip area. "I'm afraid not," was her solemn reply. Bummer! It was hard to hold back the tears (clearly a result of my heightened hormonal state).

Being seriously committed to the use of medicine to

11

manage pain during my baby's delivery, my next shock came when I learned that the town in which we lived had a shortage of anesthesiologists, so epidurals were not available. What? No drugs? Come to think of it, my husband, who was also my labor coach, might have ended up being more disappointed by this turn of events than I! And then there was the baby itself. For some reason we were firmly convinced that our first child would be a girl. Imagine our surprise when my doctor announced, "It's a boy!" I think I replied with something intelligent like, "No, it's not!" Or perhaps it was, "Are you sure?"

Because of my limited experience, I also bought into the idyllic pictures of moms with their new babies that you see in commercials and magazines—the beautifully coifed new mom who smiles lovingly as her infant nurses contentedly. Back in the real world, new motherhood was a shock. Nursing did not come as easily as touted by my breast-feeding class teacher when she described it as "the most natural thing in the world." Due to sleep deprivation, I had perpetual black circles under my eyes that rivaled my worst didn't-wash-my-mascara-off-the-night-before morning. And my hair, what was left after the postpartum fall-out, was never shiny or styled, probably because it was rarely washed.

If the physical challenges of motherhood were a surprise, I was similarly unprepared for the emotional demands of young children. It didn't take long, about a week in fact, for me to bump up against the first great contradiction of motherhood. My baby wanted me to be with him all the time, and I, well, didn't. It was only natural from my newborn's perspective—

he'd accompanied me 24/7 for the past nine months wherever I went, whatever I did. He was new to this separation thing. I, on the other hand, had thirty years' experience of doing basically what I wanted to do when I wanted to do it.

Needless to say, I was a bit unskilled in exercising the qualities that make an "ideal" mother: patience, nurturing, and self-sacrifice. Thankfully God's love and grace have enabled me to overcome some of my shortcomings, but I still find myself wondering from time to time, "Is this what I should be doing with my life, Lord?" Most often this question comes to me at times like this morning when I had finally sneaked off for a shower, alone, only to hear a little person calling "Mommy" through the door just as I'd lathered up my hair. In response to my query of "What do you need?" my youngest son answered, "Nothing, I'm just waiting for you."

"Isn't that sweet," you're probably thinking. I thought so, too, once I got over being dismayed that I couldn't seem to finagle five minutes to myself. Being on call twenty-four hours a day is not my style, and that is how I know God has me right where He wants me. Because the only way I can handle the non-stop requirements of motherhood is by turning to Him. "My soul finds rest in God alone; my salvation comes from him. He alone is my rock and my salvation; he is my fortress, I will never be shaken" (Psalm 62:1–2).

"My soul finds rest in God alone." Rest—physically, mentally, and spiritually—is hard to come by when you are a mom. I think I've already established that I can't even find it in that most personal of places: the bathroom. (Although I do always have my best prayer time in the shower.)

We know our bodies need rest. As a mom you may have hit that physical wall where your body responds to sleep deprivation, or simply too much busy-ness, by manifesting symptoms of illness. It forces you to sit down, or lie down, before you fall down. In our earnest quest to be everything we can to everyone and to do everything we can for everyone, we tend to forget that even the Lord rested on the seventh day after creation.

We crave rest mentally and spiritually as well, and God promises that we may have it. "Come to me, all you who are weary and burdened, and I will give you rest. Take my yoke upon you and learn from me. . .and you will find rest for your souls" (Matthew 11:28–29). As a mom, the key to finding rest lies in figuring out how to claim that promise for ourselves while balancing the ever increasing demands of family.

You may have heard the term "multitasking." Who is it that wired moms so they can simultaneously cook dinner and disengage themselves from a telemarketing phone call while their preschooler flies around the room making photon-laser cannon noises? God, of course! He designed us for this VIP title of "Mom." Even the creators of Superman didn't give their superhero such powers! While treading in this chaos, my daily salvation, as well as any patience and concentration I can muster, comes straight from the Lord.

I don't pretend to have all the answers for handling those times when you feel like locking yourself in the bathroom. But I do know that God can meet you in there just as surely as He could on a beautiful mountainside or in a chapel. In fact, I think God is the reason why family life is filled with so many moments of fun and silliness: your baby putting his sock on his head because it makes you laugh or your preschooler making up her own jokes that are so nonsensical they're funny. God inserts these moments of humor into our days as mini-breaks, if we take the time to recognize them as such. It's easy to get so caught up in everyday tasks that we miss the joy of being together. Raising children should be fun, right?

The Lord also knows a mom's need for separateness—even when she is tied to an infant's feeding schedule or cuddling a toddler struggling with stranger anxiety. That's why He has instilled in us the desire for solitude and the need to replenish that part of ourselves which is not absorbed by family responsibilities. God understands our craving for a break. And He gives us that much needed time so we may renew our desire to "shepherd" those He has placed in our care; not just because their needs demand our attention, but because we want to give it freely.

As wonderful and rewarding as parenting is, it doesn't take long for a new mom to realize something that we all know but rarely admit: Being a mom is tough! But making time for yourself while doing "the hardest job you'll ever love" can be even tougher. That's what this book is all about. My hope is that these pages will help you move past those times when even the bathroom offers no sanctuary, so that you may emerge to the next stage of motherhood with your sanity and salvation still intact.

Getting Away from It All

Very early in the morning, while it was still dark,
Jesus got up, left the house and went off to a solitary place,
where he prayed. Simon and his companions went to look for him,
and when they found him, they exclaimed:
"Everyone is looking for you!"

MARK 1:35–37

Life certainly would have been easier if my children had arrived with an instruction manual. Being inexperienced, I equated my first baby's cries (of which there were many) with bad mothering. So I spent every one of Baby #1's waking moments trying to make sure he cried as little as possible. I know; it's a ridiculous notion. If only someone would have told me point-blank, "Babies cry. It's normal!" But they didn't, so the first time around I wore myself ragged walking, rocking, and swinging. Thank goodness I overcame that aspect of my Supermom complex by the time Baby #2 arrived.

My first child seemed to become particularly agitated if my attention wandered to personal matters like taking a shower or even going to the bathroom. Many days I'd cross my legs and wait anxiously for my husband to get home from work so I could take a potty break! Looking back, it is exceedingly embarrassing to have denied myself the time to satisfy even the most basic of physical needs, not to mention that I gave so little credit to my child's ability to adapt to a few minutes alone.

I could empathize with my baby's need to be with me as much as possible. But I hadn't counted on just how long that stage actually lasts. I thought that by the time my child started walking, he would also outgrow his desire for us to be joined at the hip. Then I could resume a slightly modified version of my pre-mommy life. Of course, the reality couldn't have been more different. Before Baby #1 had stopped clinging, I had another baby, and somewhere in the ensuing craziness of caring for two children under the age of two, I lost my former life. Or rather, I lost myself in motherhood. When I had the time to think about it, which was rare, letting go of my previous identity was pretty scary.

Just about the time I thought I'd be able to find a few minutes for myself, it actually became more difficult. At the end of babyhood, a mom faces the double whammy of shorter nap times combined with her child being mobile. Before my child began to scoot we engaged in "parallel play" with me working on a project while my baby played nearby. But once he became a toddler, any similar effort inevitably turned into a demolition derby instead. It is hard to overestimate the number of things a boy in the toddler stage can break, smash, or tear.

Some of my friends have locked themselves in the bathroom (à la "Calgon, take me away") to get a break from their little darlings. That never worked for me. Whether I hid in the bathroom, bedroom, or closet, my kids could hunt me down and flush me out in record time. However, I did find a way to make myself invisible for short periods of time by introducing my children to the game of hide-and-seek. When I needed a few minutes to myself, I would hide in a really hard spot on my turn. Even though I was usually folded up like an accordion, two things about this game were appealing. First, I could actually sit alone for a few minutes, but more importantly, listening to the kids search for me always made me smile.

Perhaps I do have difficulty setting appropriate boundaries for my kids, but I have shared this struggle with enough other moms to know I am not alone. When my children were all preschoolers, the only time to myself I could count on was (don't laugh) while mowing the lawn. No matter how loudly one would come to tattle on another, I could smile and legitimately feign deafness over the noise of the mower. I never minded cutting the grass!

Even now, as when Jesus "got up, left the house and went off to a solitary place" (Mark 1:35), I can sneak out for an evening walk—leaving our children in the very capable hands of their father—and return to three kids and a dear hubby greeting me at the door with "Everyone was looking for you!" Getting away from it all when you have young children is not easy.

Each mother has a different tolerance level for the amount of time we spend with our children, just as each of us has a unique level of tolerance for labor pains, the number of toys strewn about the living room floor, and how many times we ask for dirty clothes to be placed inside the hamper instead of in front of it. An acquired skill in mothering is the ability to go over the top even when your upper limit has been reached. We think we can't read *Goodnight Moon* one more time, but we do. We cringe when our child pulls out the Candyland game, but we play—again.

Still, the desperation to briefly escape the responsibilities, work, and noise of a growing family can make a mom consider some pretty far-out possibilities for getting away from it all. For me, the most extreme example came on a road trip from Texas to our home in Illinois. The passengers were myself, my mother, and my three children (then ages four months, four years, and six years old). Mom and I thought it would be easier to drive all night rather than stop, unload, and try to sleep in a hotel. So everyone was tired and cranky, especially the adults.

Only a mere hour and a half from our house, the older kids were bickering, the baby was crying, and my mother sat in a virtually comatose state. We entered a highway construction zone, and I neglected to slow down. I'm not sure what the highway patrol officer thought when I rolled down my window and the noise spilled out to him, but he decided to take pity on me after surveying my situation. Not, however, without first employing what he thought would be a scare tactic.

"Do you know that I could take you to jail for driving ten miles over the posted limit in a work zone?" he asked. It may have been my hopeful gaze that prompted him to give me a warning instead of a ticket. Or maybe he could read my thoughts: Do I get my own cell? Is baby-sitting available? At that moment, a few hours to myself under any circumstances sounded really good. Have you ever felt that jail was preferable to spending more time together? Or perhaps that family time has become a "sentence" you would rather avoid? It doesn't take this extreme level of family togetherness for a mom to feel like she needs a break—daily life is wearing enough.

My friend Anne has a completely different opinion about spending time in the car: "My sanctuary was my car. Even if I had to wait until my kids were all asleep, I would go out and drive around by myself for awhile—just me and some music on the radio. Thank goodness a local convenience store was always open, so at ten or eleven o'clock at night I could still say, 'I have to go to the store for some milk for tomorrow morning.' Sometimes I'd have a good cry before I came back. That was my personal 'therapy' session, in the automobile."

The Bible speaks of Jesus spending time alone and going off to a solitary place, usually in order to pray. "After he had dismissed them, he went up on a mountainside by himself to pray. When evening came, he was there alone" (Matthew 14:23). Or as in Matthew 14:13, "he withdrew by boat privately to a solitary place." What it must have been like for Jesus! People constantly clamoring around Him, everyone wanting to talk to Him, touch Him, ask for His help—even His disciples. In a way it sounds like being a mother, doesn't it?

As much as He wanted to reach everyone, Jesus knew His limits. He recognized the importance of reconnecting with His Father for direction, support, and encouragement. He accepted the necessity of taking time to renew Himself— in mind, body, and spirit. Jesus provides us with the perfect model for taking time to nurture ourselves. I sometimes think, if the Son of God took time for reflection and prayer, could my need be any less?

Of course, just as it was with the multitudes in Jesus' time, my own brood resists any attempt for me to get away. For the longest time, my very verbal daughter would follow me wherever I went, talking the entire time. If I went into the bathroom she followed me in. She would still be talking, through the closed door, after having been gently ushered back out! That kind of dogged devotion is touching, but also exhausting.

Sometimes we need an outside source to help us recognize our need to get away. When my friend Tina's boys were ages one and three, a visit from her own younger brother provided a wake-up call that she needed a break. Her brother had stopped by to enjoy lunch with his sister and nephews. Before she handed him his plate, Tina carefully cut up her brother's pears into bite-size pieces. When he saw what she was doing, her brother said, "Tina, you really have to get out more!"

So how does a mother with a growing family get away from it all? Any way she can! We would all love to spend a day at a spa or go on a weekend getaway to some exotic locale. But most of us can look forward to that type of escape, say, once every five years. Mothers with young children often struggle to carve out any time, or even space at home, for themselves. Any attempt will likely involve either juggling a baby-sitter's schedule (if you can find one) or installing some sort of child-containment device like a baby gate or child-proof door handle. The sheer amount of effort required to get some time to oneself is daunting. Thank goodness you don't actually have to leave to get away from it all.

To reenergize themselves, moms in this season need a K.I.S.S. (Keeping It Short and Simple) time-out. I mentioned earlier that the shower is my special prayer spot. It's actually my best place for thinking of any kind—my most fruitful ideas, insights, and inspirations come to me there, even with interruptions. A shower get-away (or bath, if you prefer) is the perfect example of a K.I.S.S. time-out for a busy mom. It fits into the daily schedule. No special equipment or supplies are required. And it can be as short as you need it to be, depending on the size of your children and your water heater.

Here are some other ideas for K.I.S.S. time-outs:

- rub lotion onto your hands and feet and
  give them a massage

- read a daily devotional or meditate on
  inspirational quotes

- plan a project you would like to do, even
  if you can't start yet

- arrange some flowers from your garden in a
  small vase

- make a cup of tea and watch the activity
  outside your largest window

- call a friend and compare your day

Do anything that gives you pleasure, even if it is uncon-
ventional. A friend of mine especially looked forward to one
day in the week when she could catch up on current events
in the world "outside."

*When my children were young, I remember that
Newsweek magazine came on Tuesdays. The postman
brought it with the rest of the mail at 10:00 a.m., and
I would lay it on the table in plain view as my motiva-
tion to get the kids down for a nap. I used to read it
cover to cover before they woke up. It was my only link
to the outside world.*

What about getting away from it all spiritually?

Scripture reminds us to "turn to God, so that. . .times of refreshing may come from the Lord" (Acts 3:19). Spending time communicating with God—either in prayer or by simply making yourself still in order to hear His voice—refreshes our hearts, minds, and souls. God can work miracles with just a few minutes!

Jesus knew He needed solitude to renew His mind, body, and spirit in order to continue caring for those around Him. Having time to myself, whether for an hour or a day, allows me to recharge, which translates into more energy for my family, so that even when life is chaotic (which is most of the time), I can respond to their needs in a positive manner. Sometimes getting away keeps me from running away!

Mom's Moments

Plan how you can spend time by yourself this week: get up early, sit down during naptime, put a "Do Not Disturb" sign on your bedroom door for thirty minutes, or go for a walk alone after dinner.

At least once a month, get away from the house by yourself for an activity you enjoy.

Carve out a space of your own to get away from it all, even if it's just a corner of your bedroom or a small desk and chair. Make a rule for your personal space, "No toys or other family clutter allowed."

Kids Say the Darndest Things

Before a word is on my tongue you know it completely, O Lord.

PSALM 139:4

Cooing. Babbling. Crying. It takes many months for our baby's attempts at communication to become intelligible. Then comes the momentous day when he or she utters that first word. My husband and I waited excitedly and competitively. Would our son's first word be "mama" or "dada"? After much coaching from each of us, we had our answer. His first word was "dog" (but "mama" was second).

It is comforting that the Lord, at least, knows what kids are going to say. From that first word, it was apparent that my husband and I could not presume to know what would come out of our children's mouths. Funny, insightful, cute, embarrassing—their speech has not disappointed us. Like when our youngest child's big brother was singing to soothe him:

> *Yankee Doodle went to town riding on a pony,*
> *He stuck a feather in his hat and called it macaroni,*
> *Yankee Doodle keep it up, Yankee Doodle Bambi. . . .*

Or the time I was preparing to nurse the baby and my daughter exclaimed, "Here comes the milk bar!"

When kids are little, their lack of verbal skills can make it hard to know what they are thinking. My youngest son used to growl like a dog whenever another child bothered him. His immediate family members knew what "Grrrrrr" meant, but it seemed to perplex his playmates. When young children do speak, their innocent and often hilarious comments give us insight into what is going on in their heads. Young children's verbalizations help them interpret their thoughts and experiences; through speech they are making sense of their world. My kids, at least, like to "talk things out," endlessly. Yet verbal communication has so many subtleties—one word may have several different definitions, and the way a phrase is spoken can change its meaning. How confusing it must be for them at times! Those misplaced words and misused phrases are the basis for many keep-it-in-the-family jokes. Here are two from the journals of my friends:

> *I had been stuck at home for several days with two sick*
> *preschoolers, and my cupboards were getting bare. One*

morning when the worst was over, my three year old asked, "What are we going to do today?" I replied, "We are going to the store without fail." My son asked, "Who is fail?"

My older daughter asked one day why we were telling her younger sister Gwen, who was in the midst of potty training, that she was "doing a good job." I said, "We always give Gwen praise when she goes to the potty." My older daughter replied, "We don't give her praise, we give her toilet paper."

Some of a child's most interesting interpretations relate to matters of the spirit. On one hand, it is difficult for them to comprehend the intangible concepts of faith, but on the other, they are blessedly free of preconceived notions and teachings, misguided or otherwise. Because a child's experience is so limited, it is important for us to be as clear as possible in matters of faith—and be prepared to answer a lot of questions!

A mom I know shared a story about a nephew of hers who was confused about the priest's instruction at confession. The youngster confided to his mom, "He told me to say two 'Our Fathers,' but I only know one." Another friend's son listened closely to the pastor's preparations for communion, in which there were several references to the "body of Christ." Finally, her little one couldn't contain himself any longer and blurted out, "I can't stand it! Where is the body of Jesus Christ?" Even the pastor had to smile.

While kids refine their verbal skills, we often act as interpreter to others who are unfamiliar with their unique dialect. There have been times when even I could not understand what my children were trying to communicate—a frustrating situation for both of us! It's encouraging to remember that interpreters of all sorts figure prominently in Scripture. For example, the ability to interpret dreams was greatly valued in biblical times. When Joseph was imprisoned in Egypt he was asked on several occasions to interpret a dream. The first time Joseph replied, "Do not interpretations belong to God?" (Genesis 40:8). He agreed to provide an interpretation only because he knew God would reveal the meaning to him.

Sometimes our children's interpretations of the things they hear can point out spiritual truths, even to us. One of my friends had coaxed her reluctant son into sitting at the table to practice writing his name. (Of course, he would rather have been outside playing.) After much complaining, he wrote his name a couple of times, then looked up at his mom and said, "Mom, you know even God rested on the seventh day." To which she replied, "Yes, but God didn't get a bad report from His preschool teacher about His handwriting." Without missing a beat her son replied, "Only because God is perfect and we are sinners." Not knowing what else to say, his mom let him go out to play.

Many of our preschoolers' comments are simply uninhibited observations about the world around them. On a family vacation trip to the Grand Canyon, a friend's youngest daughter complained, "What's the big deal? It's just a big hole!" That's certainly one way to look at it. While driving through town during high school football season my own daughter asked, "Mommy, do we have to throw toilet paper all over our house, too?" We can forget that young children see things in very simplistic terms—until they put those perceptions into words.

Have your child's innocent observations ever pointed out something that is lacking in your life—like taking time out for yourself? When my daughter was four, she told a friend of mine, "When I get older, I'm going to have scratchy legs just like mommy." I know her statement was meant as a testimony of love and devotion for me, but thank goodness my friend was also a mom and could relate to not having the time to shave her legs for weeks at a time!

After my sister-in-law and her family moved to a new town, she was too immersed in unpacking boxes and helping her preschoolers settle in to find a new hair salon. It was only after her daughter observed, "Mommy, you look like a skunk! You have that big stripe down the center of your head!" that she realized her dark roots were in serious need of lightening. She found a new beauty parlor pronto.

Sometimes kids' observations reveal deeper issues in our lives. One mom who works in a bank related her conversation with a little girl waiting in the lobby along with her mom and two younger sisters, "You look so pretty today in that dress. How does your mother manage to have you and your sisters looking so nice?" The girl replied, "Well, she cries a lot." This child's comment reveals how intently our kids observe what we say and do, how quickly they internalize our words and actions into their own lives. My youngest son recently told me, "Mommy, you're stressed out. You need to take a break." Talk about observant—my five year old knew I was ready to blow before I did!

Our children's words can also give us a reality check, an indication, from their unique perspective, of how we are doing in our mothering. Are we meaning what we say, and saying what we mean? A friend put her three-year-old son in his first time-out for the recommended three minutes to discourage some inappropriate behavior. Days later she discovered her "punishment" had been misinterpreted by her son (and so was completely ineffective) when he asked, "How 'bout we play that game 'time-out'?" Obviously some further explanation was needed!

Do you know a child with a flair for dramatic or manipulative behavior? Kids learn quickly that the things they say illicit responses from us, both positive and negative. They can bask in the laughter generated by an off-the-cuff comment like this one: A father asked his five-year-old daughter to pick something up off the floor. She sighed and said, "I just wish I was four again"—as if life goes downhill once you turn five! Children will use their own personal brand of kiddie logic to try to convince you to let them do things their own way:

My mom was trying to get my daughter to take a nap

even though she wasn't really a napper. Mom tried everything she could think of. Finally, exasperated, she said, "Honey, you need to close your eyes." To which my daughter replied, "My mother lets me go to sleep with my eyes open." All my mom could say was, "Okay?!"

The first unkind thing my son said to me came in the form of a comparison to a villain from the Disney story *101 Dalmatians.* He was angry because I wouldn't let him do something he was intent upon doing, like poke the dog with a fork, so he said the ugliest thing he could think of: "You're a mean lady, just like Cruella De Vil!" I sneaked off to the bathroom for a short cry. It might have turned into a longer cry if I had realized that the phrase "you're mean" was actually a comment on my character—one that my children revisited on at least a weekly basis. They knew intuitively that casting me as the villain would hurt, and sting it did. Reminding myself that no one had labeled me "mean" since a disagreement over a toy in my own preschool years helped to put these juvenile attempts at manipulation into perspective and also rescued some of my self-image.

Children are consummate imitators. Our own well-meaning words, when filtered through a child's naive interpretation and repeated to others, can make us want to hide in the bathroom. A company my husband worked for decided to close its doors, leaving him to search for a new job. The economy was in one of its periodic downturns, and my husband was a bit worried about finding another position quickly. Trying to spare my husband's feelings, I talked with our young son about why daddy would be home more and why his mood might not be the best. A few days later my son and I were waiting in line at our bank to make a withdrawal. When we reached the counter, my son told the teller in a conspiratorial tone, "My daddy's sad because he lost his job." I'm sure she checked our account balance carefully before giving me the cash. I quickly learned that while honesty is the best policy, full disclosure is often not necessary, or prudent, with young children. Do you think these lyrics were penned more for a child or for the adults surrounding a child?

Oh, be careful little ears what you hear,
Oh, be careful little ears what you hear,
For the Father up above is looking down in love,
So be careful little ears what you hear.

Humorist Will Rogers wrote, "Try to live your life so that you wouldn't be afraid to sell the family parrot to the town gossip." When it comes to our own speech, children seem to have a gift for picking out that one inappropriate word spoken in a moment of weakness, pain, or anger and using it for maximum shock value. My friend Lisa relates this story about her two-year-old daughter:

I took my daughter to the doctor for a routine checkup
that followed a visit when the doctor did a throat swab
to check her for strep. That previous visit had been a
horrible experience, so my mother insisted on coming
with me this time because she was certain she could

make my daughter, the apple of her eye, be reasonable.
After waiting in the office for what seemed like hours
with a scantily clothed child, the doctor finally walked
in. My daughter took one look at him and started
screaming, "Don't touch me @#$^%!" My mom was*
just mortified, but the doctor said, "It looks like her lan-
guage skills are right on target." My mom never offered
to go to the doctor with me again!

Obviously, that was language Lisa didn't want the family parrot, her daughter, repeating. "Do not let any unwholesome talk come out of your mouths, but only what is helpful for building others up according to their needs, that it may benefit those who listen" (Ephesians 4:29). I'm sure the author of this passage, Paul, is referring to cursing and other inappropriate language when he mentions "unwholesome talk," but there are other things we say to our kids that can be just as damaging. The rest of the verse talks about "building others up" to "benefit those who listen." Our children take to heart the comments we make both to them and about them to others. According to Dr. James Dobson, "A sizable portion of your child's self-concept emerges from the way he thinks you 'see' him. He is more alert to your statements regarding his worth than on any other subject."[1]

As an unseasoned first-time mom and incurable perfectionist, I was rather hard on my oldest child. Knowing that negative labels could be very damaging, I tried not to use them, but criticism crept into my language more often than I would like to admit. "That's not the way you do it." "I don't think you're trying very hard." The labels were never spoken, but my child was certainly smart enough to know they were implied (and of course, the Lord knew they were in my mind).

It hurts to hear my child reprove himself now, often too harshly, for minor mistakes or lapses in judgment. Our unwholesome words from the past are very hard for children to overcome. I wish now I had considered my comments more carefully and voiced only those that would have built my children up and met their needs for unconditional acceptance and affirmation!

"My tongue is the pen of a skillful writer" (Psalm 45:1). What are our words writing into the book of our children's days? Sure, it's hard to always say the right thing in the heat of the moment, but Scripture reminds us to "stop thinking like children. . .in your thinking be adults" (1 Corinthians 14:20), a fact often forgotten when we are angry or hurt. We are the adults in this relationship and are therefore held to a higher standard in thought, word, and deed. Children do not have the life experience we adults have accumulated—life experience that mitigates many of the negative things we hear. So moms need to temper their words with TLC.

- Think before you speak. Many of a child's actions or comments do not require an immediate response. There is usually time to step back and consider what to say.

- Listen to what your child says to understand his unique feelings and perspective. You may have to do a little digging to uncover the underlying cause to an "effect."

- Choose your words carefully. Will what you are about to say harm or help your child? Remember, we should say what will benefit our children according to their needs, not our own instinct to lash out or criticize.

Moms benefit from using this technique, too. Just as putting a smile on your face eventually makes you feel better (even if you don't mean it at first), putting a positive tone into our interactions through the use of TLC tends to make our own outlook more upbeat as well. Just think of the reduction in "mommy guilt" when you no longer have to agonize over things you've said to your child in haste or in anger!

"He who loves a pure heart and whose speech is gracious will have the king for his friend" (Proverbs 22:11). Obviously these are traits each of us should aspire to model—having the one who is sovereign over our lives not only as our Lord but as our friend! Scripture speaks clearly as to how much damage an unbridled tongue can cause, and in no relationship is this more true than with our children. God calls us to do more than avoid unwholesome language. Our words to our children should be gracious and spoken with TLC.

Would you be embarrassed for your family parrot to talk to the town gossip? If you aren't sure, reflect on what your child's words are telling you about their observations and interpretations of your life together. Kids really do say the darndest things!

Mom's Moments

If you haven't already, start keeping a journal of the funny things your child says. Even the most awkward outbursts can become fond family memories when you look back on them later.

Are there certain trigger situations, or even times of day, when you find it hard to guard your mouth and tongue? (Proverbs 21:23). Come up with a plan for handling those instances so your words instruct and heal rather than hurt.

Write verses from Scripture like the ones below on "sticky" notes and post them around the house to remind yourself to use your words wisely.

Psalm 34:13—Keep your tongue from evil.

James 3:5—The tongue is a small part of the body, but it makes great boasts.

Proverbs 12:6—The speech of the upright rescues them.

What Goes in Must Come Out

(Though not Necessarily the Way You Expect)

You discern my going out and my lying down;
you are familiar with all my ways.

PSALM 139:3

Have you noticed how the focus of conversation with other adults changes once you become a mom? Talk starts to center around something we wouldn't normally discuss in polite company: bodily fluids. Moms obsess over what, and how much, they can coax kids into eating, as well as the form and frequency with which it comes out. Many developmental milestones of childhood relate either to something going in or something coming out, so keeping track of a child's bodily fluids becomes a mom's new pastime.

With young children there are so many decisions to make, and each one seems momentous. Then, for every decision, we have to convince our child that our choice is the right one. My first big decision was breast versus bottle. For me, breast-feeding seemed the natural choice. I was staying at home, and health care professionals touted the slogan "breast is best." But in all honesty, breast-feeding was not as easy as my childbirth coaches made it sound—and this is coming from a three-time breast-feeding mom.

Whether it was the way I held them, or the fact that their little noses were particularly stuffy on one side, or that they harbored some deep-seated preference for the right or the left, from time to time each of them would only want to drink from one breast and not the other. The result was a decidedly uncomfortable lopsidedness. With each child there came at least one time I felt so frustrated that I wanted to give up. But for my husband's encouragement, I probably would have. Then there was the leaking whenever I heard a baby cry—my own or someone else's. And finally weaning.

The plan was to breast-feed each child for six months and then switch to a bottle. Only one of my children decided to go along with the plan. My first child refused to take a bottle of any kind, ever. He was weaned directly to a sippie cup after eleven months of nursing when my doctor insisted I stop because I was pregnant again. All this makes it sound as though my experiences with breast-feeding were not positive, but overall, they actually were. Making that decision helped show me there are many ways of parenting, and that more than one choice can be the right way, especially if what you choose is the right decision for you and your child.

A conversation I had with another mom while waiting at the pediatrician's office confirmed this perception. She confided her fear that her child's recurring ear infections were caused by feedings from a bottle instead of the breast. I hope I was able to soothe her worry by telling her that my eleven months of breast-feeding had no effect on my oldest son's tendency toward ear infections. We, too, were at the doctor's office every other week! Even though our approaches were very different, this Mom and I ended up in the same place with our kids.

For newborns and infants, what goes in is wholly linked to what comes out. Comedian Bill Cosby once performed a routine where he talked about the changes in his and his wife's main topic of conversation after their first child arrived. They became inordinately enamored with the contents of their child's diaper, her "poo-poo." They would show each other the "poo-poo." When their own parents came over they would show them the "poo-poo." Who would have thought an interest in stools would be one of the universal experiences of parenthood? As Cosby points out, parenting transcends both educational levels and social status.

Diaper changing came as a complete surprise to us. I had

only changed a couple of diapers in my lifetime prior to our first child coming along, and my husband had never changed any. We had no idea a baby boy's "fountain" when relieving himself could be strong enough to reach halfway up the wall and accurate enough to hit us square in the face. Life can be stranger than fiction! I found myself wondering if Mary, Jesus' mother, ever had these kinds of concerns and experiences when He was a baby. Is that what is meant by "[He] is familiar with all [our] ways?" (Psalm 139:3).

Just as we became comfortable with the first phase of feeding and changing our baby, the next big milestone loomed ahead: solid food. The usual excess of conflicting parenting advice confounded this decision as well. My mother encouraged me to start my first baby on solids as soon as possible. This was largely because, at four months of age, he still wasn't sleeping through the night. Then I had all those parenting books telling me to wait as long as possible to avoid problems with food allergies. My pediatrician weighed in somewhere in the middle of these two points of view. So at around four months, my son had his first taste of oatmeal. He actually grabbed the spoon on its way to his mouth for a second bite and never looked back. (But he still didn't really sleep through the night until he was nine months old.)

Ever the dainty little girl, it took my next child about another month in the developmental scheme of things before she really began eating solids. Unfortunately, that didn't stop me from trying to force her into her brother's routine. I remember her sitting in the high chair crying because she didn't want to eat and me sitting across from her and also crying out of frustration. "Let us not become weary in doing good, for at the proper time we will reap a harvest if we do not give up" (Galatians 6:9). Finally, I realized I was the one with the problem. Obviously, it was not the proper time for her to start solids. I was once again reminded that the "right" way to do things is not an absolute but a moving target based on the differing needs of my children.

How do you know when to begin giving your baby solid foods? Wait for signs that she is interested. Does she watch you eat? When her eyes follow your food as it moves from your plate to your mouth, when her hands reach out to grab your food, and when she is able to sit up in a high chair and join you at the table, then it is time for solids. Babies should be fed according to their own developmental skills rather than a pre-set calendar or clock.[2]

Food—glorious food. Switching to solid food opens up a whole new world for moms and babies. Food on the fingers, food in the hair, food on the clothes—we quickly learn that, yes, it is possible for kids to wear more food than they actually eat. And if changing our babies was a challenge when they were very young, things become even more interesting once they start eating solids. I confess to hiding out in the bathroom after announcing, "Your turn!" when my husband was home and a particularly odious smell came from a diaper.

One of my biggest moments of panic came in changing my youngest son's diaper the day after his "Blue's Clues" birthday party. To celebrate the big event we had served a cake with blue icing, some kind of blue soda, and blue gelatin cut into shapes. The contents of his diaper were, you guessed it, BLUE. Ahhhh! Wracking my brain, it took a minute or two for me to realize that blue food coloring must be one of those compounds that passes through the body. That was Blue's last clue.

Our children's eating habits can drive us crazy. Rarely do they eat what we would like, when we would like, and as much as we would like. As kids get older, they often gravitate toward a certain favorite food. Sometimes that one food is just about all they will eat. For my oldest it was macaroni and cheese—not from a box, of course, but homemade. Our second child, the naturally thin one who looked like E. T. the Extraterrestrial when undressed, has always loved lettuce mixed with salad dressing. Our youngest would eat peanut butter and jelly sandwiches three times a day, every day, if permitted. My own mother tells of the time she took me to the doctor because my skin had developed an orange tinge. It turned out my unusual coloring was the result of eating so many carrots, my favorite food as a child.

According to pediatrician Marianne Neifert, "Once a child is able to feed himself, it's time to step back and relinquish some control, difficult though this may be." Dietitian and author Ellyn Satter encourages parents to make a variety of healthy food available, but she urges parents not to assume responsibility for getting their child to eat them. "[This] advice is based on studies showing that young children who are offered a healthy menu will eat enough food over time, although the size and composition of individual meals may vary dramatically."[3] That's good news! Now we can stop the begging, threats, and flying airplane noises during mealtime, and perhaps we can get something to eat ourselves.

These changes our children are constantly going through and putting us through can be very confusing—all the more so because of the wealth of information that is available. Even after you've consulted your pediatrician, talked to your mom, read books, and researched the web, it is difficult to feel confident about the mothering choices you've made. But we can lay these questions and misgivings before the Lord. "Let us then approach the throne of grace with confidence, so that we may receive mercy and find grace to help us in our time of need" (Hebrews 4:16). Though we may feel unsure about our parenting skills, we can be confident that God is listening to our prayers. He is the only one who understands completely both our needs and our child's. Our heavenly Father can give us peace about each developmental step we take together.

"The fruit of the Spirit is love, joy, peace, patience, kindness, goodness, faithfulness, gentleness and self-control" (Galatians 5:22–23). There are few times when patience and self-control are as much of an issue for both moms and kids as during potty training. Once again, everyone has an opinion—from the view espoused by generations past that kids should be out of diapers by the time they are two years old to today's more relaxed belief that moms should wait until kids are ready. No matter which approach you choose, well-intentioned comments will probably be made. The additional pressure of being really tired of changing stinky diapers will also play into your decision.

A study by the Medical College of Wisconsin in Milwaukee uncovered these statistics, which helps put this process in perspective:

· Toilet training children takes an average of eight to ten months.

· The average age of completion is thirty-five months for girls and thirty-nine months for boys.[4]

Irrespective of the results of this study, most moms still feel as though they earn gold "mommy" stars if their kids are potty-trained before age three. If saying good-bye to diapers early means we are Supermoms, putting off training until after a third birthday (or simply failing abjectly before then) must indicate we are lazy, inattentive, or worse, ineffective. Given this bias, what self-respecting mom would intentionally hold off on getting out that package of Pull-Ups?

With my first child, a.k.a. the test subject, I started potty training when he was two-and-a-half years old, urged on by well-meaning advice and the fact that I then had two children in diapers. It wasn't long before I realized we had started too early. One morning my son had been stubbornly sitting on his little toilet for about twenty minutes while I alternately tried humor, persuasion, bribes, and threats. During a break in the inaction, while changing my daughter's diaper, I watched my son nonchalantly saunter into the bedroom closet. From my position at the changing table I asked, "What are you doing?" "Playing," he answered. When I went in to check, I found the long awaited "poo-poo and pee-pee" on the closet floor. I wanted to go lock myself in the bathroom!

After that incident we put away the potty chair for awhile. I began to understand that my child would give up his diapers when he was ready, and not a moment before. A mom whose daughter attended a toddler playgroup declared that the four kids decided to rebel and formed a "diaper support group" when potty training began. At least it seemed that way to the moms, because three of the four children were not potty trained until they were four years old. Talk about friends of a feather flocking together!

My friend Cheryl confessed how a lack of patience on her part was not helpful in convincing her daughter to give up her diapers. "I was so desperate to have my second child out of diapers that I foolishly let a neighbor talk me into trying the 'potty training in a day' technique. I lost my mind for twenty-four hours, and it didn't even work! I remember sitting there doling out little candies while holding the plastic doll that wets, thinking, 'I am out of my mind!'" (In all fairness, other moms have told me this technique worked like a charm.)

Here's a ray of hope for those immersed—literally and

figuratively—in potty training: All these kids were out of diapers, with no accidents, by the time they reached kindergarten.

The end of a matter is better than its beginning, and patience is better than pride. Do not be quickly provoked in your spirit, for anger resides in the lap of fools. (Ecclesiastes 7:8–9)

There are two things to consider before beginning potty training: Is your child ready? Are you? Kids give clues about when they might be ready to start potty training. They stay dry for longer periods of time, can get undressed well enough (and quickly enough) to make it to the potty in time, and are actually willing to sit on the thing as long as needed to get the job done. I've known moms who delayed potty training because they knew that present or upcoming circumstances would prevent them from being able to devote the proper amount of time and patience to the endeavor—reasons like a future move, a new baby, or a job change. In these cases, choosing patience truly is better than pride, and a lot less messy, too!

When you feel both you and your child are ready to begin, use whatever technique will be most appealing to your preschooler. That might mean buying new underwear with their favorite characters on them, giving a small candy reward each time they use the potty successfully, putting stickers on a chart toward earning a special toy or outing with mom—or any combination of approaches.

The downside of potty training for us was that neither of

my boys finished before that thirty-nine month mark. However, the upside to them taking their time was that they had perhaps two or three "accidents" apiece, and that was all! My precocious daughter potty trained herself at two-and-a half-years old, but her mishaps were more frequent and occurred over a longer period of time than her late-bloomer brothers. The end of potty training is always cause for celebration, and it will eventually come, irrespective of how hard you and your preschooler struggle with it. As with each developmental milestone, depending on your attitude and approach, you have the opportunity to make your child feel confident and capable or inadequate.

God has made each of us into unique individuals, and He may indeed be the only one familiar with all our ways. As moms we worry—have we made the right choices? Have we done what is best for our babies? Yet Jesus reminds us, "Who of you by worrying can add a single hour to his life? Since you cannot do this very little thing, why do you worry about the rest?" (Luke 12:25–26). Even with all the books we read and prayers we offer up, moms may not know if their decisions are the right ones. We may not know for many years to come—or we may never know, but God's Word tells us there is no point in our worrying. The Lord frees us from continually second-guessing our decisions so that we may enjoy our children in every stage, regardless of what's going in or coming out.

Mom's Moments

Give yourself a break from talk about bodily fluids. Go out to lunch or dinner with a friend (or your hubby). Make an agreement beforehand to discuss anything BUT children.

A woman of God said, "True holiness comes wrapped in the ordinary." Consider how the Lord blesses you even as you attend to the ordinary, everyday tasks of caring for your family.

Learn to take all parenting advice with a grain of salt. While you can get some of the best suggestions from other moms, that advice must always be applied within the context of your child's individual personality and developmental needs. Don't fall into the "one way or the highway" trap.

Making a Joyful Noise

Speak to one another with psalms, hymns and spiritual songs.
Sing and make music in your heart to the Lord, always
giving thanks to God the Father for everything.

EPHESIANS 5:19–20

Our home is noisy. We have a dog, phones, two boisterous boys and a talkative daughter, a washing machine, doorbells, cats, lots of sound effects, TVs, and sometimes, music. I grew up in a musical household. Although neither of my parents played an instrument, music serenaded us from the stereo for hours each day. Still, I have never been much of a songbird; my singing is best confined to the shower or car. In other words, I sing where I can be alone—and then I sing with gusto, because I love music.

According to writer Thomas Carlyle, "Music is well said to be the speech of angels." One of the pleasures of parenthood I looked forward to was introducing my children to music. From the day they were born, we listened to all kinds of tunes: classical, inspirational, kids' choirs, jazz. The only sound they didn't like was rock-and-roll—go figure. I would tell the story of the nutcracker prince as we listened to *The Nutcracker Suite*. We would cut a rug to burn off energy while listening to Big Band music.

Have you ever heard the phrase "music soothes the savage beast"? To get her kids to quiet down in the evening, one mom I know turns off the lights and bursts into song. While running errands, I discovered that one of my children could be soothed by nothing less than music. My youngest child couldn't stand riding in the car as a baby. From the moment I strapped him into the car seat until his seat harness was unbuckled he screamed at the top of his lungs. The only thing that calmed him was my singing one specific song, "Do-Re-Mi," a melody from *The Sound of Music* intended to teach the children in the story the notes of a musical scale. No other song would do. My older children quickly caught on and would begin singing, "Doe, a deer, a female deer, Ray, a drop of golden sun. . ." before I could get the key in the ignition. We had our own version of the Von Trapp Family Singers—the Singing Sumners.

After becoming a Christian as an adult, I felt embarrassed at my lack of knowledge of Scripture. A friend from church encouraged me to listen to Christian music on the radio as well as from cassettes. "Most songs are based on verses from the Bible," she advised quite correctly. So with my children, I started a collection of Bible and inspirational songs that we could listen to, sing to, and learn from together. Teaching our children to love and rely on God is our greatest moral and spiritual responsibility. "Come, my children, listen to me; I will teach you the fear of the Lord" (Psalm 34:11). What better way for them to learn than through verses from Scripture and stories set to music? After all, those messages set to music are often the ones we remember into adulthood.

One of the most joyful ways to praise and worship our Creator is through song. Whether your voice lends itself to a stage or the confines of your own shower, God loves to hear you lift it up to Him in love. Psalm 8:2 tells us, "From the lips of children and infants you have ordained praise." Through music we can teach even the smallest child to praise the Lord. You will be amazed how quickly your preschooler can learn a simple song like "God Is So Good" by singing it together. (It's a good reminder for adults, too!)

God is so good,
God is so good,
God is so good,
He's so good to me.

I've seen how the Lord blesses those who make noise joyfully. Remember my baby who cried nonstop while riding in the car? He has grown into a mellow preschooler with a sunny disposition, and he loves to sing. Christmas carols are a favorite—he evens hums them in preschool, somewhat to the chagrin of his teacher. For our family, listening to music is indeed like hearing the speech of angels. (Of course, we are not yet at the stage where we have to monitor lyrics for inappropriate content or tell anyone to "Turn that down!")

As you would expect, music is not the only sound you'll hear at the Sumner house. Our kids and noise go together like peanut butter and jelly. It didn't take long for them to realize that the louder they cry, scream, or babble, the more likely they are to get attention. That's not so bad when you have just one little person in the house—the parent-to-child ratio is manageable. But when you have three young children (or more!) all employing the "loudest child will get the most attention" principle, it's hard to think, much less figure out what anyone wants!

Moms are entangled in a Catch-22. We want our children to communicate openly with us, but there are times when all we long for is peace and quiet. For women like me who were used to existence at a lower decibel level, the increase in volume can be exhausting and nerve wracking. Like the Grinch in Dr. Seuss' *How the Grinch Stole Christmas,* my head starts to ache from "all the noise, noise, noise, noise."

There is one particular situation that pushes every mom's buttons: constant interrupting. The act of talking to someone else, whether on the phone or in person, is like turning on a magnet. Children are attracted to you from all over the house. No matter how adept you are at multitasking, it's natural to lose the thread of a conversation with someone else talking to you at the same time—especially when the voice is coming from the general vicinity of your knees.

Often my kids just can't wait to tell me what's on their minds. A friend gave me this positive alternative to their verbally interrupting. If a child has something urgent to say (and everything is "urgent") while I'm on the telephone or talking to someone else, they put their hand in mine or on my arm. Then I know to stop my conversation as quickly as is reasonably possible so I can find out what he or she wants. The payoff with this approach is not that your children quit coming up with urgent things to tell you, but that you don't have to hear "mom, mom, MOM!" each time.

For my children, riding in the car is the prime time for making nonstop noise. But I've learned I don't have to be held hostage by their desire to communicate or make spaceship-jumping-to-hyperspace sound effects. At an early age they were all introduced to the "quiet game." The first one who talks or makes a sound of any kind loses. I reinforce the benefits of winning by keeping a box of special snack treats in the car. Sure, there are crumbs in the seats, but at least I have some peace and quiet.

I've already mentioned that our family tends to be, well, loud. But there's one time in particular when the decibel level rises sharply—just about the time my husband comes home from work each day. Some moms refer to this daily period of craziness as the "arsenic hour." Fussy babies, fighting preschoolers, a frazzled mom trying to fix Tater Tot casserole—late afternoon is unquestionably the noisiest time of day. Dad's arrival home just adds fuel to the fire—especially since he is rather loud, too. For some reason he objects to being "shushed" or told to use his "inside voice" instead of an "outside voice." Given the chaotic nature of this time of day, I am sometimes amazed he comes home at all!

Commiserating with other moms has taught me a lot about coping with the dreaded arsenic hour. The first tactic I learned was to lower my expectations (and my husband's) about what would be served for dinner. Meals that take longer than thirty or forty-five minutes to prepare are off the menu. A man of great wisdom said, "Better a dry crust with peace and quiet than a house full of feasting, with strife" (Proverbs 17:1). Sandwiches, with crusts or without, are fine most nights if it means everyone is less stressed.

A little thought to arsenic hour entertainment goes a long way toward diffusing tension. Most preschoolers are very intent on "helping." Set a pot on the counter with a little water in it and give your preschooler a spoon to stir so they can cook, too. (They may need to stand on a stool so they can reach.) When my sister and I were young, my mother would even let us sprinkle some spices into our pot to make our "water soup" a bit more realistic. Young children are also very interested in raw ingredients. Give your children a celery stalk or whole carrot to investigate as you chop pieces for dinner.

Keep a special toy bag to pull out when you sense a potential meltdown. Fill it with inexpensive, non-messy toys to be used only at this time of day. This is also an excellent time to let your child pull all the Tupperware out of the cabinet. Make a game of putting it back after dinner. If all else fails, turn on some music and boogie while you bake!

Not all the noise at our house is joyful or even pleasing. We have our share of angry outbursts, both the kids' and mine. Anger is something we often avoid talking about in Christian circles. To admit that we get angry is tantamount to admitting that we lack self-control and are sinful, not to mention "bad" moms. The Bible even tells us, "Everyone should be quick to listen, slow to speak and slow to become angry, for man's anger does not bring about the righteous life that God desires" (James 1:19–20).

Remember when you couldn't conceive of getting angry with your little darling? I recall gazing down at my first beautiful newborn, a miracle resting in my arms, and thinking, *How could anyone get angry with such an angel?* It doesn't take long to realize another great contradiction of motherhood: You can love your child fiercely and be intensely angry with him at the same time. Even with infants it is natural to feel exasperation, or perhaps a little anger or frustration, at the cries that awake you for the third time in three or four hours.

When my oldest son went to preschool, I was fortunate to make friends with a mom whose son was in his class. We were both devoted to our children, but after spending some time together, I began to feel there was something wrong with me. We all enjoy a honeymoon of sorts after our children are born, a period of time where they can do no wrong. (And indeed, they can't really do anything wrong as infants.) This phase lasts longer for some moms than for others—my friend was obviously still experiencing it, though my honeymoon period had started to fade. With difficulty, I listened as she went on and on about her smart, adorable, and well-behaved son. As I struggled to deal with my #1 wild child, I rationalized, *Two out of three qualities isn't bad.* I was way too intimidated to talk to her about the occasional anger I felt toward my son.

Why are moms so afraid to talk about their anger? The word "anger" alone appears in my Bible 256 times. If you add the variation "angry" the total goes up to 372, and that number doesn't include "rage," "wrath," or "fury." Obviously, the Lord recognizes that anger is an issue for us. There are plenty of Old Testament references to God being angry. Perhaps it is not the fact that we are angry that frightens and shames us—so could it be what we do when we are angry instead?

The philosopher Aristotle wrote: "Anyone can become angry—that is easy; but to be angry with the right person, and to the right degree, and at the right time, and for the right purpose, and in the right way—that is not within everybody's power and is not easy."

In fact, only God exhibits perfectly righteous anger, an emotion that is expressed yet never controls or dominates His actions. I certainly can't claim that same power. So how will I ever lead a righteous life if I can't keep from yelling at my preschooler when she knocks over a glass of juice?

"In your anger do not sin" (Psalm 4:4). The Lord wants us to differentiate between anger and the actions that stem from our anger. When talking to our children about a misdeed, psychologists tell us to separate the behavior from the child. In other words, you should tell your child, "I'll always love you, but hitting your little brother is not okay." Similarly, moms must realize that anger is a normal human emotion, a feeling we may not be able to prevent and must sometimes accept. However, we have the choice to either give in to our anger or to control it and refuse to commit a sinful act.

There have been moments in my children's young lives when I have raged out of control—until a moment when I see "that look" on their faces. It's a look of fear; they don't know what mommy will do next and don't want to find out. That look stops me dead in my tracks every time as I reflect: What am I doing? How can I act threateningly toward someone I would give my life for?

"A fool gives full vent to his anger, but a wise man keeps himself under control" (Proverbs 29:11). A frustrated mom admitted to trying her own version of primal scream therapy on one occasion when her anger flared. "I remember screaming when a couple of my kids were having matching hysterical hissy fits—I was screaming with them, not at them. They were so surprised they quieted down for a minute." A warning to those of you considering this technique: If sufficiently startled, your children may stop their own screaming momentarily, but they can always outlast you in the screaming department.

There are many other techniques to manage this kind of anger, but the bare essentials come down to three steps. The first thing to do when you feel anger rising inside is to stop. Tell yourself to "stop," leave the scene for a few minutes, or count to ten or twenty—anything to stop the emotional buildup. Next, think about the underlying reasons for your anger and how to handle the situation productively without damaging your child's spirit. Finally, respond in the way you feel is most appropriate. One approach that helps me respond more civilly is another mom's suggestion to treat my kids when we are alone as I would if we were out in public. Aren't we usually on our best behavior when others are around (even if our kids aren't)? By taking the time to first stop and think, my response to their misbehavior is usually more rational and appropriate.

It is easier to follow these steps if you have spent time in advance planning how to handle various situations you may encounter with your child, particularly if you have communicated the potential consequences to them. For example, if you think your child may break into a tantrum in the checkout line at the grocery store, tell her before you start shopping that a tantrum will result in consequences of XYZ when you get home. (A reward for good behavior might be in order, too!) Then follow through based on your child's actions.

Did you know that most tantrums actually serve as an outlet for your child's strong feelings? Those outbursts are expressions of their inner struggle for self-control. Our children are not usually trying to embarrass us when they choose to throw a fit in a public place—regardless of how intentional their down-on-the-floor, red-faced, non-stop screaming display appears. Reading about child development or taking a parenting class will help you develop realistic expectations of your child's behavior based on her developmental abilities, and that can help you diffuse unjustified anger.

Is there anything good about losing one's temper? I can think of one thing: Losing it gives us the opportunity to teach forgiveness. If the expression of your anger has hurt your child, it is essential to ask for his or her forgiveness. Talk to your child about how the Lord forgives us when we do something wrong and how He expects us to do the same. "Forgive, and you will be forgiven" (Luke 6:37). As you ask for their forgiveness you will be teaching your child how to take responsibility for his own behavior. Admitting your mistake and saying, "I'm sorry" is the only way for the forgiver and the forgiven to live in God's peace (Colossians 3:13–15).

The words of the psalmist at the beginning of the chapter demonstrate wisdom for living life—even though the topic of anger is not specifically addressed. Can you yell or rage in anger while singing and giving thanks to the Lord, either out loud or in your heart? For me, those two possibilities are mutually exclusive. By remembering to always give thanks to God for everything—for the noise, the interruptions, and the angry outbursts—we, together with our children, can make beautiful music together.

Mom's Moments

Keep some CDs on hand with songs you can sing to. If the volume level gets too high at your house, don't crank it up further by yelling. Turn on the music instead.

Seneca, a Roman philosopher, wrote, "The greatest remedy for anger is delay." If you feel an irrational or dangerous level of anger toward your child, now is a good time to lock yourself in the bathroom and take some of those deep, cleansing breaths you practiced in childbirth class. Remain in the bathroom until your anger is under control.

Anger can be triggered as a response to negative events in your past. Take a hard look at whether your child's behavior is reawakening any childhood trauma of your own, and seek help from a pastor or counselor if the problem is out of control.

"Rest Time" and Other Misnomers

This is what the Sovereign Lord, the Holy One of Israel, says:
"In repentance and rest is your salvation, in quietness
and trust is your strength."

ISAIAH 30:15

At our house there were two typical "rest time" scenarios. In scenario #1, I coaxed my baby's and preschoolers' tired little bodies onto their respective beds and tore around the house like the Energizer bunny—picking up toys, doing dishes, sorting laundry, and returning phone calls. Scenario #2 proceeded with me announcing it was rest time and my kids running around the house like the Energizer bunny (with me in hot pursuit), all the while tearfully asserting they were not tired.

Scenario #1 was much more common when my children were very young. At least then they would sleep some during the day. But those daytime naps were catch-up times for me— a chance to get some of the day's work done so that I'd be free when my little darlings woke up and demanded my full attention. As my children grew older, scenario #2 days became more frequent because I had the amazing non-sleeping kids. By the time they were two years old, they were avoiding rest like the plague.

I tried to continue our tradition of an afternoon "rest," but no amount of threats or promises would keep my kids in their rooms. Our pediatrician suggested placing a baby gate across the doorway to help contain them. And it did, for a day or so, although they tended to look a bit like those little puppies for sale at the pet store. They would hang on the gate and watch me go with those big, sad eyes. A few days later, after they learned how to knock down the gate, I tried an alternate suggestion: closing the door and securing it so they couldn't escape. Bad idea! I tiptoed up to check after ten minutes to find the room looking like a tornado had hit and my son asleep on the floor underneath the toddler bed.

I heard a story of one mom who actually installed a screen door onto the doorframe of her son's room. He couldn't get out because it was locked from the outside, but he was calmer because he could see out, and mom was calmer because she could see in.

Whoever coined the term "rest time" probably was not a

mom. For most of us, that time of the day is anything but restful. We continually put aside our need for downtime in favor of getting one more thing done. We put aside the need but can't escape it, physically, mentally, or spiritually. What's a mom to do when she knows she needs "rest time" and her kids insist they don't?

First, take some godly advice. Our Lord is so wise! The Bible tells of a special covenant He made with His chosen people; He made the seventh day, the Sabbath, a day of rest. "For six days, work is to be done, but the seventh day is a Sabbath of rest, holy to the Lord" (Exodus 31:15). God established this covenant as a means for His followers to demonstrate obedience, but also, in effect, to save them from themselves—to legitimize the concept of rest. I can just see the Old Testament women, hands on hips, repeating, "God said we have to rest today," when their husbands asked about dinner. The observance of the Sabbath allowed all family members, their servants, and work animals time for relaxation and restoration. "Anyone who enters God's rest also rests from his own work, just as God did from his" (Hebrews 4:10). The Old Testament even prescribes time for farm land to rest—special time for it to lie fallow from planting to recover its richness and fertility.

Our own personal, physical need to rest was also recognized by Jesus. "The apostles gathered around Jesus and reported to him all they had done and taught. Then, because so many people were coming and going that they did not even have a chance to eat, he said to them, 'Come with me by yourselves to a quiet place and get some rest'" (Mark 6:30). (By the way, when was the last time you had a chance to eat without hopping up to grab this or that for another member of the family?) Jesus saw that the apostles were in need of some downtime to be physically renewed. Today's super-charged society has definitely gotten away from the practice of resting.

That exemplary and sometimes intimidating description of a wife and mother of noble character we learn about in Proverbs 31:28 says, "Her children arise and call her blessed." Of course, this means they must have been asleep first, before they could "arise." If there's a baby in your home, the first step to finding personal rest time is to persuade him or her to sleep. Often that isn't as easy as it sounds, but here are some suggestions to make naptime and even bedtime more comfortable for baby:

- Make sure neither of you is disturbed by sudden noises. Turn off the telephone ringer, put the dog out to avoid spontaneous barking, and put a note on the door asking visitors (and delivery people) NOT to ring the bell.

- If your baby tends to awaken easily, use a "white noise" machine that produces unobtrusive, calming background noise, play a recording of quiet, soothing nature sounds like ocean waves, or even turn on a fan—anything that makes repetitive, monotonous sounds to drown out other noise will work well.

- The most desirable bedroom temperature is
  around 70 degrees with a relative humidity of
  about 50 percent. Check to make sure your
  baby's room isn't too hot, too cold, or too
  stuffy to rest comfortably.

Several moms I know, desperate for their little ones to nap, resort to going for a drive and allowing the car to lull the youngsters to sleep. Then they carefully bring the baby carrier inside for the remainder of rest time. Every time I tried this strategy, my babies' eyes had a bad habit of popping open as soon as the engine was turned off, but some moms make this approach work well.

Another rest-time option is to read books to them. My friend Tina employed this tactic:

> I had a stack of Little Golden Books that I'd read before I put the boys down for a nap. If my younger son wasn't quite asleep, I'd even read the list of other book titles on the back cover. That would usually do it. All he really needed was to hear the sound of my voice for just a little longer.

With your child finally "down" in his or her bed, the next challenge is to sneak out of the room without them getting up again. I remember on many occasions crawling out on my hands and knees so my drowsy but not soundly asleep child wouldn't notice me leaving. As Tina recalls, "I don't think I even breathed. I'd be holding my breath and crawling out of the room." And woe to the mother who peeks over the bumper pad just to see an eye pop open!

For moms with older children, having regular rest time becomes more problematic. Eventually, I did have success with a couple of tactics, starting with letting my preschoolers know they did not have to sleep if they didn't feel tired. However, they did have to stay in their room until the timer I set went off. They could also listen to a story or music on tape. The end of the tape was their cue that rest time was over. If they came down before the timer or tape went off, they would have a negative consequence like missing an afternoon video or a bedtime story. There were two other components to this approach:

1. My kids had a sufficient number of fun, non-messy activities or toys in their rooms that they could play with independently to stay sufficiently occupied, and

2. I needed to monitor my own behavior so that I put a reasonable amount of time on the timer. Even if we were having a difficult day, it wouldn't do to compromise my kids' belief in the finiteness of rest time by extending it to say, two hours!

Once the kids are sequestered, you have to choose how to spend your precious time. Actually, it's a good idea to decide what to do before rest time begins in order to stay focused and avoid wasting time in indecision. Do you want to kick your feet up, close your eyes, and take a physical rest? Or do you need more of a mental rest, a psychological release from the pressures and tensions of being a mom? Do you need "rest time" or "private time"? The fact is moms benefit from both. Why do moms with young children at home need a mental rest? Sure there's a lot to keep up with, but rolling a ball back and forth and making "train coming into the station noises" to entice your toddler into opening her mouth for another bite of vegetables is not exactly rocket science.

The biggest reason most of us need mental "private time" is to take a break from the mommy guilt demon that sits on our shoulder day in and day out. What I find most interesting is that no matter what you do as a mom, regardless of the choices you make, there's always something to feel guilty about. If you have a job outside the home, you feel guilty because you aren't there day-to-day, hour-to-hour, and minute-to-minute with your little one. If you are a stay-at-home mom, you feel guilty because you aren't contributing to the family finances and fear you may be "squandering" your education and previous work experience.

A friend with three children who recently took a job outside the home has cut down on her morning "to do" list by allowing the girls to choose their own clothes for the day. Recently, she lamented, "My youngest daughter will leave the house wearing red, white, and blue shorts with a purple shirt, and I think, *You can tell your mother works full-time.* Your older sisters would never have left the house looking like that!" Mommy guilt has this mom worrying about the fashion police. I'm sure the other kids her daughter is with never even notice.

I thought I had found the perfect compromise by having, in effect, my own home business. But I feel guilty when

I turn down an invitation from a friend to go to lunch or go shopping on the weekend when I need to catch up on a writing or speaking project. My mommy guilt demon whispers negative comments when a deadline requires me to turn down my children's request to play a game and I pop in a video instead. Other moms tell me how lucky I am to have a more flexible work schedule, so then I even feel guilty about feeling guilty!

If there isn't enough about our life choices to awaken the guilt, our children can certainly get that demon talking. How about when we cave in at the grocery store checkout counter and hand them a piece of candy? Anything for a few minutes peace while you write a check and load the bags into the car! Or when we break our own rule and bring a fussy baby to sleep in bed with us for a few more minutes of shut-eye? Let's see a show of hands—how many moms out there really believe they are doing a good job in all areas of their lives, especially mothering? If your hand isn't up (don't feel badly, mine isn't either), then your mommy guilt demon may be in control.

Where does all this guilt come from? For most of us it is a natural result of wanting to do a good job at something we care so deeply about, namely being a good mother. However, in pursuing this goal we often compare ourselves with an unnatural model of the perfect mom: She is usually a composite of the best qualities of other moms we know or have read about. Her perfection is a myth because she isn't real. "My guilt has overwhelmed me like a burden too heavy to bear" (Psalm 38:4). Our obsession with this ideal can consume us. That's why it is important for moms to distinguish between the positive and negative aspects of guilt.

Sometimes there is a good side to guilt. Feeling guilty can be constructive if it leads us to recognize areas in our lives where improvement is needed and encourages us to take the steps necessary to change. But these are not the kinds of positive messages communicated by the mommy guilt demon, which instead sends messages that lead to non-productive regret. Moms who are physically and mentally tired find themselves more susceptible to the ravages of guilt but less able to consider its positive possibilities. Taking private time for ourselves without feeling guilty gives us a break from those negative messages and allows us to gain perspective on the nature of our tension and guilt.

Say you're feeling guilty because you snapped "Not right now" at your child when she asked you to crawl on the floor and play pretend mama dog and baby dog. You then proceeded to rant about how your three year old really needs to start entertaining herself.

Positive guilt: You obviously need a break. Playing like you are a dog doesn't sound so bad after you've had a rest and a chance to read the letter from your sister that came in today's mail.

Negative guilt: You lost it again. What kind of mother are you? Your daughter will probably remember that tirade for the rest of her life.

Positive guilt leads to positive action while negative guilt leads to wallowing in pessimistic, self-destructive thoughts. " 'Oh, that I had the wings of a dove! I would fly away and be at rest' " (Psalm 55:6). As I mentioned earlier, I had a habit of using my children's rest time to catch up on things around the house that needed doing. One day, as my children rested while I washed dishes and looked out the window, I daydreamed, "If I had wings, I'd fly to Cancun and rest on the beach!" Obviously, that was not a realistic break, but I could use rest time to take a mini-break.

I like to think of a mini-break as something you would do if you were on vacation, but without the hassle of making reservations, packing up all the kids' stuff, and actually going away. You'll need a spot where you feel comfortable and a basket or box of mini-break "supplies" to keep on hand. Stock your basket with something soothing or refreshing to drink like herbal tea or special juices in small bottles, a CD of relaxing and inspirational music, a "stash" of your favorite treat or snack, scented lotion, and a paperback copy of a book you've always wanted to read. Tailor the contents of your mini-break basket to your unique interests. Make the first thirty minutes of your child's rest time your own quiet time of renewal.

There are days, however, when we've had enough of being by ourselves. To combat feelings of isolation there's just no substitute for adult companionship. Motherhood can feel like the loneliest job you'll ever do, which is why most moms identify with this psalmist's prayer at one time or another: "Turn to me and be gracious to me, for I am lonely and afflicted. The troubles of my heart have multiplied; free me from my anguish" (Psalm 25:16–17).

Spending time with family members is an expedient balm for the feelings of loneliness we all experience—expedient because your mom, sister, or grandmother are all intimately aware of your past and present situation. You don't have to bring such family members up to speed on who you are—they've already seen you at your best and your worst. I'm always comforted when I tell my mom about my latest mothering challenge and she responds, "Don't worry, we had that same problem with you." (Conversely, I try not to panic when she says, "I don't know what to tell you. That never happened to us.")

Families don't usually have to plan anything special when they spend time together. Most family members are completely satisfied with the opportunity just to shoot the breeze. For me, there's a comforting continuity in sharing family stories. How can we know where we're going if we don't know where we've been? When my almost one-hundred-year-old grandmother tells stories of taking a bath in an outdoor wooden tub with homemade lye soap and recounts how hard her mother, widowed at an early age, worked to ensure the family's survival, I am very thankful for the private time I can find.

Maintaining friendships with other moms also gives us the opportunity to sound off—to laugh, cry, complain, rejoice—in order to keep the troubles of our hearts from overcoming us. Never underestimate the power of girl talk to refresh you emotionally! Private time spent during rest time may be the only chance for moms to reconnect with friends, at least without having to worry about being constantly interrupted. If you are still having trouble setting aside dedicated private time to chat on the phone, try some of these options to avoid feeling isolated and losing touch with your friends.

- Send postcards. Faraway friends can still be a part of our friendship circle. Mailing a postcard is a fun and fast way to keep in touch (and more personal than E-mail).

- Go for a walk. Ask a friend to join you for a walk before your children get up in the morning or walk together after dinner when someone else can watch the kids.

- Join a group. If you've recently moved and need to meet new friends, join a group that shares your interests, like a book discussion group, mom's group, or Bible study.

I've belonged to a book discussion/therapy group for the past six years, and I don't think I would still be in one piece without it. Each month when we get together, at least one (or two or three) of us plops down in our seat and says, "I really need this tonight." We almost always find time to actually discuss our latest book selection in between sharing the latest happenings in our lives. Whether we see each other during the rest of the month or not, I count these women among my closest friends. They are my comic relief, my support staff, and my extended family all rolled into one. My friends free me from the anguish of loneliness—thank goodness I don't have to do motherhood without them!

One more type of rest is essential for moms: spiritual rest. "Quiet time" has become the current terminology for time spent in prayer and meditation. It has a nice ring to it, don't you think? But if rest time is hard for a mom to come by, quiet time is twice as tough. Spending meaningful time with the Lord is difficult not only because it involves finding or making the time, but also because we need to be still enough in our hearts and minds to hear and respond to Him.

The Lord tells Moses, "My Presence will go with you, and I will give you rest" (Exodus 33:14). God is always waiting for us to turn our minds to Him. While His presence constantly surrounds and envelops us, we must be tuned in to "ask where the good way is, and walk in it" so we can find rest for our souls (Jeremiah 6:16). Even when we do sit down alone for twenty minutes, the inner tranquillity we need to enter God's rest may not automatically appear.

There have been more times than I would like to admit when I have sat down on the couch with my Bible study guide in one hand and a pen in the other, feeling I was ready to commune with the Lord. And nothing would happen. Slightly frustrated I'd think, *Okay God, I'm here. Where are you?* Perhaps that particular Bible study didn't move me, or I couldn't stop thinking about an argument I'd had with my child earlier in the day, or sitting on the couch was more conducive to watching TV than studying Scripture. Whatever the reason, my heart wasn't ready to enter God's rest, and without that readiness, my quiet time was empty.

Regardless of distractions and other obstacles, strengthening our relationship with the Lord is important in this busy season of our lives. We each encounter crises in our mothering journey where all our experience and abilities seem useless for the task at hand. Time spent with God prepares and empowers us to deal with these crises—it creates intimacy, trust, and confidence in Him for us to draw upon. Without this time, God may be speaking, but we will not be listening.

If you are having trouble connecting with the Lord, consider trying a new way to relate. Spend your quiet time outdoors, or choose some other place where you are drawn near to Him. Meet God through music or art or through reading some of His Word and meditating on its meaning in your life. Attending a Bible study or bending our knees in prayer are not the only ways to grow with God. Find a new place or method to interact with Him that fits your unique personality, because only then can His Spirit guide you to the rest that is a mom's salvation.

Mom's Moments

Don't become a casualty of the "mommy wars." Since there is plenty of mommy guilt to go around, be a positive influence in the life of another mom by offering to help her with errands or watching her kids. Be willing to accept an offer of help if you are the one who needs it.

"Let us draw near to God with a sincere heart in full assurance of faith, having our hearts sprinkled to cleanse us from a guilty conscience" (Hebrews 10:22). Have you approached the Lord recently and allowed His love to cleanse you?

Keeping a journal allows you to express your innermost thoughts and feelings without fear of judgment. According to author Crystal Bowman, "A personal journal can also be spiritually therapeutic. Writing prayers, poems, or spiritual thoughts gives you some solid material to go back to when you are facing trials and need some encouragement."[5]

Fearfully (and Wonderfully) Made

For you created my inmost being; you knit me
together in my mother's womb.
I praise you because I am fearfully and wonderfully made;
your works are wonderful,
I know that full well.

PSALM 139:13–14

Before our children were born, we were so anxious to find out what they would be like. We had nine long months of speculation. Would it be a boy or a girl? Have my green eyes? Share my husband's and my wavy brown hair? Did the fact that the baby inside me woke up kicking and rolling every morning at 3:00 A.M. mean he had his days and nights reversed? (Yes.)

Finally, mom, dad, and baby were formally introduced. I'll spare you my birth stories; suffice it to say that each of our children arrived in their own unique way. And my husband and I began the lifelong journey of getting to know our offspring. Isn't it amazing the way God creates such variety within our families—how each child is a staunch individual with unique traits and temperament? Some kids give you a glimpse of these characteristics from the day of their birth. With others, the process of discovering their true identity takes longer.

"Before I formed you in the womb I knew you, before you were born I set you apart" (Jeremiah 1:5). The Lord knows our children's personalities long before they are born. And it seems to me that, from the beginning, He has put siblings who are of opposite temperaments and personalities together. Take for example the story of the first brothers, Cain and Abel—Abel was a shepherd; Cain was a farmer. Abel worshiped God with the best he had to give; Cain brought only what he had on hand and wanted to spare. You know the rest. Cain allows his baser instincts to control him and kills his brother (Genesis 4:2–8). This is the first case of the "good son versus bad son," of siblings who come from opposite ends of the spectrum, and it appears in only the fourth chapter of the Bible! Despite their differences, God knew and loved both of the brothers even before they were conceived by their mother, Eve.

We have opposites in our family, too. Once he decided he was hungry, our first child could not wait for a meal. Any dawdling on my part—like to heat up his food—would cause him to fuss until he quickly became too hysterical to eat. To this day he has issues with delaying gratification. On the other hand, his brother would sit in his high chair and sing happily while waiting for his food to arrive!

At the same time, as a preschooler our oldest son was not the least bit picky about other matters—like where he chose to relieve himself. One day while we were outside planting flowers, he ran from the front yard toward the back. Since he didn't answer my calls, I followed him to find out what he was up to. As I rounded the corner of the house, I found my little boy "watering" the lawn. I'm sure he thought he was being discreet, but he had chosen to face our neighbor's house instead of our own, much to the amusement of the elderly woman living next door.

Our usually more mellow youngest son was surprisingly uptight about this particular issue. While on a very long car trip, at the furthest point between the last bathroom we passed and the next, he decided he needed to use the facilities "right now." We weren't in the middle of Nowhere, but in our current location there wasn't a bathroom for miles. As we hadn't seen another car for the past twenty minutes, we pulled over to the side of the road and suggested he go au naturel. Guys usually enjoy that kind of thing, right? (At least our oldest child did.) A few crocodile tears quickly gave way to a full-blown meltdown—he refused to go to the bathroom anywhere but in a bona fide toilet! Since we had just finished with potty training, I had stashed his potty chair in the back of the car before we left as an afterthought. After our son used the "facilities" we were back on the road again.

As we drove away I reminded myself that there were worse vices than an overdeveloped sense of modesty.

Other moms have observed striking dissimilarities in their kids, too:

Tina: *One of my boys would pull out all the pots and pans from the cupboard each day. His brother was content to sit and color or do puzzles.*

Cheryl: *My oldest daughter, Samantha, did everything and got into everything, and she was never happy about any of it. She would be the one coloring all over the walls so that you had to repaint. Her younger sister, Ashley, comes along and doesn't touch a thing. Doesn't open a drawer. Doesn't touch a cabinet. And she smiles her way through everything. I think she was too involved watching Samantha. My youngest daughter, Jorie, is like the perfect mix: into everything, doing everything, and happy to do it!*

These differences between our children are largely superficial in nature. While their individual preferences contribute to sibling rivalry, I have no doubt that it would exist even if they were carbon copies of each other. She's on my side! His piece is bigger! Mommy bought me this, and she didn't get you anything! What a perfect world this would be if I only had to deal with one child at a time.

When I go shopping with just one child, we usually have

a good time. When I bake cookies with one child, I get to feel like Betty Crocker and Mother Goose rolled into one. When I sit on the couch to read to just one child, we snuggle together and enjoy the story. Whenever I spend time with just one child on his or her own, we both have a good time. Compare this to time spent with more than one child. While shopping at the grocery store, one child is always either trying to climb into or out of the cart while the other tries to "help" by attempting to run them down, knocking canned goods from the shelves in the process. Baking cookies together becomes a fierce competition first to see who can get the most cookies on their sheet and secondly to see who can dump the greatest amount of decorating sprinkles on top, rendering the cookies inedible to all but those under the age of six. Reading to more than one child at a time turned into a game of who could get in the best punch, pinch, or kick, all the while with you-know-who (me) right in the middle of the action. All the fighting would make me want to run up the white flag and head to the bathroom for a truce.

I may not have the troubles Eve faced while raising Cain and Abel, but I never left my firstborn alone with his sister, who is nineteen months younger. I wasn't exactly sure what he would or wouldn't do, but his behavior at the time led me to believe that it might not be pretty! (Thank goodness he grew out of that phase by the time baby #3 arrived.)

The Lord certainly understands the lengths brothers and sisters will travel in order to get the upper hand. Another biblical story of two brothers, Esau and Jacob, includes all the elements of sibling rivalry we see played out in our own homes: jealousy, deceit, anger, and fighting. Jacob deceived his father in order to receive the blessing reserved for the oldest son, Esau. Esau burned with a murderous rage that only dispersed after Jacob lived for many years in another land. I have observed my children as well as others take things from one another according to the Toddlers' Creed, "If I'm holding on to it, it's mine!" Older, craftier preschoolers will temporarily convince a younger sibling that he or she doesn't want a coveted object—only to run to me in anger and indignation when their little brother or sister asks for it back. I imagine God feels his kids are fighting all the time, too, just like in our home.

How can we encourage our children to get along and appreciate one another rather than antagonizing each other? As mothers we need to recognize the importance of making this point with our children. "Even a child is known by his actions, by whether his conduct is pure and right" (Proverbs 20:11). Getting along with others is a life skill every person should possess, and encouraging this ability in early childhood increases the chances the behavior will "stick" as kids grow. Besides, who better to practice on than your own siblings?

If your children have trouble playing together without a serious confrontation, you may need to observe their interactions for awhile. Start by showing them how to be kind. Ask them to use words, nice ones, like "please," when they want something that someone else has. If they cannot stop fighting over a toy, give them a real-world consequence—take the toy away or send both of them to neutral corners.

Setting boundaries with your children can benefit you as well as them. When your children are old enough, let them know you do not like to listen to quarreling. If they cannot play peacefully, they must go to another room. This tactic often cuts back on arguing since it removes one of the biggest rewards: tormenting you.

With the birth of our second child we had a matched set, a boy and a girl. Having grown up at a time when both men and women were being liberated from old stereotypes, I had accepted the theory that males and females were basically the same. The old thought was that differences in the ways girls and boys were raised accounted for the variations in our thought processes and lifestyles as adults. My first two children gave me a lesson in genetics. Yes, environment and upbringing contribute greatly to a child's behavior and interests, but there are also basic fundamental differences between the sexes, even in our earliest years! God celebrates the distinctive traits He gave each of us, including differences in gender. Knowing that His "works are wonderful" has helped me appreciate my children's unique qualities.

What are little girls made of?
Sugar and spice, and everything nice,
That's what little girls are made of.
What are little boys made of?
Snips and snails, and puppy dog tails,
That's what little boys are made of.

—Old Nursery Rhyme

Our son is a typical boy: boisterous, high-energy, disorganized, fond of bugs and snakes, and not fond of craft projects unless they involve making a really big mess. He takes what I consider a disturbing amount of pleasure from both whacking and stomping on things, and he is able to correctly duplicate the sound effects from any movie he watches. On the other hand, my daughter is a typical girl: verbal, high-energy (so much for stereotypes), extremely organized when she wants to be, loves small furry animals including puppies and kittens, and could care less about playing cars or imaginary games involving weapons and commands like "kill." She enjoys doing arts and crafts activities but not cleaning up afterwards, and she will help me around the house as long as it's her own idea.

Though I have tried to treat each child in the same way, their individual actions cry out, "I gotta be me!" Before each subsequent sibling was born, I took each of my "big" kids to the toy store to pick out a doll to care for as I attended to our newborn. Even though my son was too young to feel any social pressure about playing with a doll, he was very reluctant to choose one. Indeed, after a cursory inspection of it at home, he never touched it again, preferring to play with his cars and trucks while I changed, fed, and bathed his infant sister. My daughter loved the idea and actually began collecting "baby" dolls to care for.

Generalizations are dangerous and often inaccurate—I see this among my own children. In our family, the boys tend to be more interested in music and books, while my daughter is an accomplished athlete. Research has shown that there are physiological and behavioral differences between the sexes. Even as newborns, boys behave more aggressively than the average girl—they are less placid, quicker to cry, and more demanding.

The first playgroup I attended consisted of my son, four or five little girls, and their respective moms. It didn't take long for me to realize that my son and I were the "odd men out," to coin a phrase. For the most part, the little girls played together quietly and peaceably. They did not chase each other around menacingly, waving the hammer from the pounding bench. When the girls took away a toy from my larger, louder son (which happened frequently), the incident was somehow his fault. Thank goodness one mom in the group had an older preschool boy. She affirmed that my son was normal and behaved just as other little boys do—or I could have come away from that experience thinking there was something seriously wrong with him.

In their book *Raising Sons and Loving It!*, Gary and Carrie Oliver provide insight into some of the physiological differences between girls and boys: "When comparing male and female brain structure, girls have a larger connection between the right and left sides of the brain and are better able to access both sides at the same time." This makes it easier for girls to do things like read written material and identify specific emotions on other's faces. However, "the right hemisphere of a boy's brain is better developed than the left hemisphere," which gives him a better ability to perform spatial tasks and to focus on one task at a time.[6]

"In Christ we who are many form one body, and each member belongs to all the others. We have different gifts, according to the grace given us" (Romans 12:5–6). As moms we want to help our children develop their God-given gifts and abilities to the fullest extent possible—regardless of whether our daughters are tomboys who shun dolls and refuse to wear dresses or our sons would rather swing or blow bubbles than play ball. Here are some ways to avoid stereotyping while encouraging your child to explore his or her individuality.

- Encourage boys and girls to try whatever activity they express an interest in. Refrain from labeling any activity as "boyish" or "girlish."

- Arrange interaction with different-gender playgroups. Watch videos or DVDs where boys and girls are both represented or where gender isn't really an issue with the characters, such as in Veggie Tales.

- Help your son acknowledge and express his feelings, especially vulnerable ones. Give him the opportunity to play the nurturer or care-taker from time to time.

- Encourage your daughter to build things. Don't inhibit her desire to run around and get dirty.

So much of children's development hinges on how we respond to them: with approval or displeasure, love or indiffer-ence. After the birth of my first child, I found it inconceivable that a mom could not instantly fall head over heels in love with her baby as soon as he or she was placed in her arms. As the birth of my second child approached, I began to rethink that conviction. Could I really love another child as much as I do my son? God's capacity for love is limitless, but was there room in my human heart for another baby?

When our second and third babies were born, I learned that the umbrella of a mother's love stretches to cover each new addition. As they've grown I've found that my love and commitment to my children does not change or lessen whether they are boys or girls, good or bad, like me or complete opposites. Jesus gave us an example of this type of unqualified love in His parable of the lost son. A son leaves home and foolishly squanders his portion of his father's estate (given to him in advance). The father was still filled with compassion for his wayward son, and he happily welcomed the lost child home, going so far as to have a feast to celebrate his return. This father's love for his son was not diminished because the son abandoned him and made very poor life choices along the way! (Luke 15:24). The parable is intended to demonstrate the unconditional and unfailing love God has for each of His children—it is a model for us to aspire to in raising our own.

Perhaps one of the most difficult aspects of raising more than one child is avoiding playing favorites. My feelings towards my kids are not exactly the same, and they can fluctuate depending on the phases both they and I are going through at the time. Sometimes it's easier to gravitate toward the child that is most like me—unless that child exhibits qualities I don't like in myself. (You know, those perfectionist tendencies can be really irritating in kids!) Sometimes I'm drawn to the surprise of the child with whom I have less in common. The challenge is to let each of them know the depth of my love, even when we are not totally in sync.

Playing favorites with your children can have disastrous consequences. The Bible recounts the story of Jacob, who was the father of twelve sons and several daughters. Jacob loved his son Joseph "more than any of his other sons" and openly demonstrated his favoritism by giving Joseph a beautiful, ornate robe. "When [Joseph's] brothers saw that their father loved him more than any of them, they hated him and could not speak a kind word to him" (Genesis 37:4). The brothers plotted to kill Joseph, but eventually, they opted to sell him into slavery instead, all because he was his father's favorite. This story clearly shows how an obvious preference for one child over another breeds resentment and bitterness.

Avoid playing favorites by not making comparisons between siblings. Continually remind yourself of each child's special strengths and talents. As a visual reminder, make an acrostic based on each child's name. List their unique qualities. Hang the acrostics up where you will see them often; recognizing their unique strengths and talents will help you focus on God's wonderful work embodied in your preschooler. Often we don't realize that our actions communicate a preference for one child over another, but kids are masters at detecting even subconscious favoritism.

Consider these four parental behaviors that may be sending negative signals.

Unequal attraction. We tend to play with, and generally be more encouraging to, the child who is our favorite. What is your attention level and body language saying about whom you'd rather be with?

Taking sides. When cast in the role of referee, do you take one child's side more often? Do you automatically assume one child is the aggressor before investigating who started it?

Name calling. Using unflattering nicknames or labels seriously undermines a child's self-esteem. Kids will also get the message if you overtly criticize one more than the other.

Talking trash. Kids hear more of what we say about them to others than we suspect. Do you brag more about one child's accomplishments while only complaining about another's exploits?

If you feel the opposite of favoritism toward one of your children, make a special effort to spend one-on-one time with him or her. A little alone time may allow you to recognize and enjoy aspects of their unique personality. Try to discover similar likes and dislikes that can bring you and your child closer. Instead of applying comparative labels, keep an open mind about their capabilities. You never know how kids may turn out—as in our family where the child who had difficulty making friends became the most gregarious and outgoing of the three. Don't berate yourself for reacting differently to each child. Family therapists say that this behavior is only detrimental if it sabotages a youngster's self-esteem or sense of security.

Eventually, all parents are asked, "Do you love me as much as my brother (or sister)?" Actually, you are lucky if the sentiment is phrased as a question. At our house it's more common to hear the imperative, "You love my brother more than me!" Most often this accusation accompanies the assertion, "That's not fair!" In fact, I heard "that's not fair" so many times that I had to come up with my own pat answer in self-defense.

I sat all the kids down together and told them: "Things at our house may not always be equal, but they will be fair." If one of them needs a new pair of shoes or new underwear, I will come home with just what they need. I won't buy everyone new shoes and underwear unless they've all outgrown theirs. As my children get older they may have different bedtimes from one another—the oldest probably won't need as much sleep as the youngest. I refuse to run myself ragged making sure each one is treated exactly the same, because my children differ just as their needs differ. However, I will love each of them completely and uniquely.

I still occasionally hear, "That's not fair!" Most often it's because one or more of my children don't like what I'm doing—not because they don't understand the intent or reasons behind my decision. Sibling rivalry may not become extinct in our home, but I'm working to put it on the endangered list. By reminding each of my children of their unique position in our family, in God's plan, and in my heart, they can be assured that they are both wonderful and praiseworthy in their own right.

Mom's Moments

Encouraging someone's gifts is not just for children. Do you have a dormant talent waiting to bloom? While you acknowledge the wonderful way the Lord made your kids, don't forget yourself, too!

If you have trouble identifying with one child in particular, consider whether he or she reminds you of someone you had trouble getting along with from your past, or if you see a part of yourself you dislike. Finding the source of your feelings can help you resolve the situation.

When your children's fighting really starts to get to you, remember—most behavioral experts encourage parents to let kids work out their squabbles (as long as things aren't getting physical). Interactions between siblings teach them social skills like taking turns and negotiation. So lock yourself in the bathroom, and don't let them drag you into the fray.

Vanishing Paper Products and Other Mysteries

*"No wise man, enchanter, magician or diviner can explain
to the king the mystery he has asked about,
but there is a God in heaven who reveals mysteries."*

DANIEL 2:27

Are you the only one in your house who is apparently quali-fied to purchase diapers, replace toilet paper rolls, get tissues for runny noses, close doors, and turn off lights? In contemplating the great mysteries of life, I never thought they included such mundane tasks. However, based on the amount of difficulty everyone else in my family has accomplishing them, these little jobs I perform on auto-pilot must actually be on the same order as building one of the seven wonders of the ancient world!

My kids and I engage in an unspoken contest to see who can use paper products down to the last piece, which means it is the next person's responsibility to refill the roll, box, or stack, right? Humorist Erma Bombeck once said, "I don't know why no one ever thought to paste a label on the toilet-tissue spindle giving 1-2-3 directions for replacing the tissue on it. Then everyone in the house would know what Mama knows." Since most preschoolers can't read, this wouldn't help us too much, but perhaps our husbands could learn.

In this game of who-can-hold-out-the-longest without benefit of said paper product, I always lose, probably because I am more averse to using my sleeve or any other piece of clothing than my children. One mom shared how she had to have an overflowing toilet cleaned out because her son had used his socks to wipe his bottom—there was no toilet paper left on the roll.

Since paper products are such a regular part of daily life, and obviously something we take great stock in, many kids take a scientific interest in the properties of paper at one time or another. Do you know approximately how many pieces of toilet paper it takes to clog up your toilet? Unfortunately, I have never discovered the critical number, being called in to help only after too many pieces have been used. (A friend has taught her kids the "five-square rule" to combat this problem. Use only five squares of toilet paper after you're done going to the bathroom.) My son, the budding scientist, almost caught the house on fire one day by testing what would happen when he stuck a paper towel into a lit candle I accidentally left within reach.

A child's well-developed sense of curiosity, combined with a complete lack of decorum about "private" matters, can lead to some embarrassing situations. I would be remiss if I didn't include some stories about kids' fascination with feminine hygiene products (closely related in importance to paper products). I do this not because they are a favorite topic of mine, but because when I asked other moms to contribute their experiences in raising young children, I received more stories on this one topic than any other. Clearly, I am not the only one who struggles to keep the supplies for that time of the month to myself.

One of my own children was so enamored with tampons that he took every opportunity to dump them out of the box and use them like Lincoln Logs to build things. The problem was getting them all back in the box and discreetly putting them away when someone would stop by for a visit. Here are some other entries for the "most ingenious way for a child to use a feminine hygiene product" contest that show us how trying to be discreet can sometimes backfire:

> *One mom's daughter found a box of tampons under the sink and asked her mom what they were. Her mother told her, "Those are special tissues only mommies use." The next day her child walked up with a tampon stuck in her nose while the mom was having coffee with a neighbor. When asked what she was doing the little girl replied, "I'm just using some of those special tissues that mommies use."*

A pair of brothers topped off their homemade knight costumes with soft "helmets" made by securing Kotex onto baseball caps. (So it wouldn't hurt as much when they were knocked in the head with a sword.)

And the winner is:

A friend's sister-in-law had been teaching her pre-schooler how to set the table. One day while at the store with her daughter, the sister-in-law had to purchase some sanitary napkins. That evening she turned to inspect the job her daughter had done setting the table to find a sanitary napkin stuck to the tablecloth under each fork. "Where are the napkins?" she asked. Her daughter replied, "There weren't any in the drawer, so I used these special ones." Dinnertime was very special indeed!

"Folly is bound up in the heart of a child" (Proverbs 22:15). I look forward to the day when I can recount these stories to my much older children to show them how foolish their actions sometimes were—preferably when a date of the opposite sex is being introduced to the family.

Why kids fixate on these kinds of things is a mystery to me. But for moms, dealing with all the day-to-day details of raising a family (like restocking vanishing paper products) can make it difficult to see the big picture of mothering. What is the "big picture" of mothering? It is the creation, through work and play, instruction and discipline, of a family that communicates its love and faith to all who belong.

We've already established that being a mom is a lot of work. I once attended a workshop on time management where the speaker, a mother of three, said she counted the number of tasks she was responsible for each week—they totaled four hundred—everything from fixing dinner to clipping the kids' fingernails. Scripture addresses the way a mom gets caught up with details in the story of Martha and her sister, Mary. When Jesus visited their home, Mary "sat at the Lord's feet listening to what he said. But Martha was distracted by all the preparations that had to be made." When Martha asked Jesus to tell Mary to help her, He replied, "Martha, Martha. . .you are worried and upset about many things, but only one thing is needed" (Luke 10:38–42). Mary chose to sit and learn from Jesus; Martha was too immersed in the details of hospitality to take advantage of the big picture right in front of her. The Son of God was sitting in her living room!

Moms are more likely to nurture a vision of the big picture for their families when they can keep their heads above water and not allow the sea of household details to pull them under. The big picture is not all fun and games, but the more fun you can make it, the better off everyone will be. Over time your children can be the lifeline that keeps you from drowning in chores, which is only fair since they create the need for most of our work in the first place! Teaching children how they can contribute to running the household gives them a sense of belonging and you a needed break—some of the time.

My friend Cheryl shared this outrageous example of a child's attempt to help that went amiss:

This story happened when I had two preschoolers at home. My youngest was still taking two naps a day, so one particular morning I put her down and raced around madly cleaning the house for a women's meeting I was hosting that evening. When I finished, I thought I'd quickly jump in the shower, so I sat my older daughter down to watch Sesame Street. When I got out of the shower I checked on the baby, who was still sleeping. I then noticed a "cloud" drifting into the bedroom. It didn't smell like smoke, but I panicked and raced down the hallway to find my preschooler scooping all the ashes out of our fireplace and throwing them over her shoulder onto the furniture and carpet. She said, "Mommy I'm helping you clean. I'm doing the fireplace." The meeting was canceled, and we had to have everything professionally cleaned!

You may be thinking that the preschool years are too early to try to instill a work ethic in your children. Actually, if you start now, your timing is perfect. I like to think of the exclamation by the genie in the Disney movie *Aladdin*, "Yes, [they] can be taught!" When our preschoolers watch us washing dishes, sorting laundry, and setting the table, they don't look at these tasks as "work." Chores are just one more thing we do that they can help with! Our own attitude demonstrates to kids that work can either give us a sense of accomplishment or bring feelings of frustration and drudgery. We have the opportunity to show how our work glorifies God when we do it with a happy heart. "Whatever you do, work at it with all your heart, as working for the Lord, not for men, since you know that you will receive an inheritance from the Lord as a reward. It is the Lord Christ you are serving" (Colossians 3:23–24).

If you are unsure what is reasonable to ask your child to help with, here are some suggestions of age-appropriate tasks. (You can start training kids to tell you when the toilet paper roll or tissue box is empty as soon as you like!)

Ages Two to Four

· Pick up toys and put them away

· Clear dishes off the table (You may want to invest in some nice plastic dishes and glasses for everyday use.)

· Help empty small wastebaskets

Ages Four to Five

· Set the table

· Help put away the groceries

· Sweep the walk (especially with a child-sized broom)

· Put clean clothes on and dirty ones in the hamper

· Make their own bed

- Sort silverware and put it away (Be sure to remove any sharp knives or utensils first.)

- Dust parts of furniture without breakables on top

When teaching your child how to do a new task, give clear instructions and demonstrate what you want done. Chores involving several steps should be broken down into smaller jobs so they won't be too overwhelming. Work side-by-side with your child until they can complete the task on their own. Doing things together shows the value of cooperation, and it may encourage your child to stay with a job longer. Most importantly, a mom's standards will have to change when kids start contributing their share of elbow grease. Don't sabotage your child's earnest attempt to help out by redoing her work, and be careful not to be overly critical. Accept her personal best effort as though it truly is the best.

This may all sound well and good, but not everyone's children have an interest in home economics—or a desire to please their moms to the point where they will pretend such feelings. What if your child is more interested in dumping every toy or book he or she owns on the floor rather than picking them up? What if they have more of a bent toward shoving a peanut butter and jelly sandwich into the VCR or DVD player instead of helping wipe jelly off the table? Is it okay not to insist that kids help out?

Each of us has to choose her own battles. You may not

feel this particular one is worth the trouble, but whether it is over this subject or another, the concept of discipline will eventually become an issue for you and your child.

Anyone who has watched a crawling baby turn around and smile before going to grab the cat's tail knows that kids are born with a sinful nature. "Children, obey your parents in the Lord, for this is right" (Ephesians 6:1). This verse is really given more for us as parents when children are very young. As with any learned behavior, however, it is better to start early. You might already be an expert at employing one of the most common words in the language of mothers with young children: No. Many moms (including me during each child's first year) worry that "no" will be their baby's first word instead of "mama" or "dada."

Saying no is usually our first attempt at discipline in addition to being our first indicator of how well our child will respond. Moms with serious or sensitive children may find that saying no is sufficient to correct their child's behavior for a long time. Then there are those of us with so-called strong-willed kids, like one of my friends who said if her son heard the word "no," he knew it was worth going after. Misbehavior in children has many causes. Kids love to push our buttons, but often they act up simply because they are tired or hungry. Before disciplining them, consider the source of the problem.

Counselors and authors Dr. Henry Cloud and Dr. John Townsend suggest using a system of choices, limits, and consequences for very young children.

Choices. Allowing your child to make as many of his own choices as possible gives him a sense of control and mastery over his day. Let him choose his clothes (except when neatness and color coordination really count), which kind of jar of fruit to eat with lunch, or where in the room to build a tower of blocks.

Limits. "A man's wisdom gives him patience; it is to his glory to overlook an offense" (Proverbs 19:11). Before setting limits for your child, first make sure he is developmentally capable of complying with them. You may feel that you are imposing too many limits if you are saying no all the time. Are you merely imposing limits but not enforcing them? A limit should be important and firm enough to be obeyed. If a limit is ignored, something negative should happen, which lead us to...

Consequences. Saying no without consequences is nagging, not discipline. The most effective consequences are actions that relate to the behavior. For example, take the TV remote control out of your child's hands if she refuses to put it down or stop reading her favorite picture book until she stops pulling your hair.[7]

Discipline is a topic fraught with controversy. If I were to assemble a group of ten women in a room, all ten would probably have their own idea about at what age discipline should begin, under which circumstances it should be applied, and what discipline techniques are appropriate to be used. Add into this abundance of opinions the fact that the type of discipline which is effective varies with each individual child, and also factor in that we tend to change discipline techniques over time to accommodate the developmental growth of our kids (and quite rightly so). Perhaps one thing that makes discipline so difficult is that it is an ever changing target. Most of us have lots of "misses" before we hit a bull's-eye and find the combination of factors that work for us and also for our child.

It didn't take long for me to realize that not only was my husband shooting toward a different bull's-eye in his attempts at discipline, he was aiming at a completely different target as well. In an Internet survey, 79 percent of moms said they are the disciplinarian in charge, while 19 percent said it's dad. That's a pretty big discrepancy! Obviously, moms and dads often disagree over discipline issues—with guys tending to be more lenient about kids' behavior. (I'm not sure if this is simply a male trait or a result of their propensity toward conflict avoidance.) The variations in my mate's and my approaches to discipline made me feel even less confident that I had a handle on the subject. To top it all off, I quickly became tired of being the "bad guy" when it came to disciplining our kids. Thankfully, things did improve once my husband and I began talking through our thoughts and feelings on the subject. Now we discuss what should happen in various situations before they occur, or at least before disciplinary action is meted out. By communicating, we present much more of a united, consistent front on issues of discipline both between ourselves and to our kids.

As with all difficult decisions, God's Word is the best place to look for direction when you're not sure who to listen to or where to turn for the advice you need. Since this is such an emotionally charged issue, I'd like to focus on how the concept of discipline is presented in the Bible. What do you think of when you read the word "discipline"? These days, the term has become synonymous with punishment, but in Scripture, discipline has more to do with instruction than with punishment.

"God disciplines us for our good, that we may share in his holiness. No discipline seems pleasant at the time, but painful. Later on, however, it produces a harvest of righteousness and peace for those who have been trained by it" (Hebrews 12:10–11). Here we see discipline as a positive, something the Lord does for our own good. God's discipline is synonymous with training that produces favorable results in our lives if we accept and apply His instruction. Our heavenly Father gives an example of appropriate discipline in the way He parents us—by using circumstances and experiences that are administered in love to guide and correct us. We should instruct our children in the same way, even though it is often inconvenient and unpleasant to do so.

"Discipline your son, and he will give you peace; he will bring delight to your soul" (Proverbs 29:17). When your child is screaming his way through a time-out, peace and delight may seem a long way off. In disciplining my own kids, I've learned that the most important aspect is constancy and consistency—simply hanging in there. You must be willing to say no to the same misbehavior ten times in a row, a hundred times in a day, or however many times it takes. Good discipline means being willing to stay home when you had planned to go out. It means sticking to your guns when it is embarrassing, because training is more important than how you look to strangers or friends. Our guiding principle in administering discipline should be to use it in harmony with the long-range goal of developing godly character. It is not to be used solely in anger or for our own convenience.

So, do I have a training technique that has solved some of our household mysteries, like reminding the kids to tell me when they use the last of the toilet paper or keeping them from putting empty packages back in the cupboard? Honestly, I haven't really tried. In my big picture for mothering, those are lessons that can wait until later. I'm still trying to come up with an explanation for why, in a family where everyone is right-handed, we still have to set the table with the forks on the left!

Mom's Moments

Do your chores feel like drudgery? Try a mood enhancer to lift your spirits while you work: listen to music and sing along, or plan some kind of a treat to enjoy once you're done.

What is your big picture of mothering? Have you been playing the part of Martha and been too caught up in day-to-day details to fill in your big picture? Think of two activities you can cut back on or cut out of your schedule entirely.

Moms most often apply inappropriate discipline when they are tired or stressed. If you've recently "lost it" with your child, consider whether one of these factors could be the culprit and take steps to address your needs.

In Sickness and in Health

Be joyful in hope, patient in affliction, faithful in prayer.

ROMANS 12:12

Most of us are familiar with the "in sickness and in health" part of the marriage vow, but oh, how that same vow is called into service when we have children! I certainly never thought I could clean up so many things I previously would never had touched without the benefit of a full biohazard suit. Still there are few times I feel as much like a "real" mom as when I'm caring for a sick child. When my kids are ill, my nurture lever shifts into high gear.

In an odd way, it's nice to have an excuse to do nothing but hold my baby on my lap and rock in front of the big window. Or to sit with my preschooler on the couch and watch her favorite video. Our household routine is put aside on sick days, and I spend an unusual amount of time thinking about what my "patients" should eat. What would look so appealing that they might actually take a bite? What would soothe a sore throat or an aching stomach? What would go down and stay down?

On sick days I don't have to feel guilty that I'm not straightening the house or keeping up with work. Caring for kids when they're feeling poorly is important, so it's easier not to feel conflicted about the way I'm spending my time. Actress Meryl Streep is quoted as saying, "Motherhood has a very humanizing effect. Everything gets reduced to essentials." Truer words have rarely been spoken, especially regarding sick days. Comforting your child, dispensing medicine, and visiting the doctor often leaves time for little else.

"The Lord gives strength to his people. . ." (Psalm 29:11). What mom hasn't used that strength to act above and beyond the call of duty in caring for a sick child? Certainly I've done things I never thought I would have to do. During one particular illness, I was surprised, and dismayed, at the depths to which I sunk. The stomach flu was running through our family—like dominoes the kids succumbed one by one. Our youngest son was the last to become ill, and he had the worst case of all. The poor little guy didn't hold anything down for three days, at which point I felt it was time to call the doctor. He prescribed an anti-nausea suppository, so an hour later I found myself sitting next to a naked, ailing preschooler holding his cheeks together (not the ones on his face) until the medicine "dissolved." I needed a break, but not in the bathroom—I'd already spent enough time in there lately.

I admit that I indulged in a few minutes of self-pity. Was this really my life? How had a woman with a Masters Degree in Business Administration, and a former career fast-tracker, been reduced to this? When your mother or girlfriend reminisces about how wonderful it is raising kids, this is not one of the events they tend to share. During the cold and flu season, when a child would come to me with a runny nose, I wanted to run the other way! The other moms I know also failed to mention that kids don't usually begin blowing their own noses until between the ages of three and four, which means they wipe them on clothes, furniture, and even the walls (in the case of one of my children). Does anyone else inwardly, or outwardly, groan when they are awakened by a feverish, "Mommy!"

With young children, illness is a family affair. My friend, Anne, shared this story:

> I remember the first night we were home with our second child. Her days and nights were mixed up, so she had slept that day and was now wide awake. Our first child was deathly ill. I was soaking in the bathtub at 3:00 A.M., and everyone else—my husband and two daughters—joined me in our little bathroom. I looked up at my husband,

who was trying to help my older daughter lean over the
toilet, and said, "Someday we'll look back and we'll
laugh." At that moment it was hard to imagine when!

Sometimes we can't escape sick kids as hard as we try. While I was pregnant with our third child, our oldest came down with a serious illness which confounded the doctors. He was admitted to the hospital where, thankfully, he responded quickly to a combination of intravenous drugs. Our son was, understandably, very scared, so I spent his first night in the hospital in the empty bed next to him. The following night, the nurses in the ward, and my husband, convinced me to let him stay the night at the hospital so I could go home, spend time with our three-year-old daughter, and get some rest.

The evening did not turn out as planned. About twelve o'clock I awoke to my daughter crying. Apparently, she had contracted the flu and had just thrown up all over her pillow. We spent the rest of the night sitting up on the couch with the "bucket" by our feet. The next morning, we learned that my son could come home. My husband greeted me with a cheery, "Feel better after a good night's sleep?" I locked myself in the bathroom for a long, well deserved bath that afternoon!

All this devotion can be a double-edged sword. Like every mom I worry, "Is this high fever caused by a virus or something more serious?" But as the days at home without a break continue to mount, a feeling other than nurture starts to creep in. Can you say "stir crazy?" My husband would offer to go pick up things from the store for us, but I begged to be the one to go. While I was heading out the door to Wal-Mart, he would give his standard sendoff, "Have a good time." Instead of cynically thinking, "Yeah, right," I found that I was looking forward to it, desperately.

Your attitude should be the same as that of Christ Jesus: Who, being in very nature God, did not consider equality with God something to be grasped, but made himself nothing, taking the very nature of a servant, being made in human likeness. (Philippians 2:5–7)

When you've been at home for an extended period with sick kids, it's hard to keep up a servant heart! Family crises due to illness may be when we most need the renewal of stillness and solitude, for it enables us to continue cleaning up the messes and comforting our charges. But that's also when it's very difficult to make the time. In his book, *Celebration of Discipline,* Richard Foster describes how to find the solitude to sustain us:

The first thing we can do is to take advantage of the "little solitudes" that fill our day. Consider the solitude of those early morning moments in bed before the family awakens. Think of the solitude of a morning cup of coffee before beginning the work of the day. . . . There can be little moments of rest and refreshment when we turn a corner and see a flower or a tree. . . . These tiny snatches of time are often lost to us. What a pity! They are little moments that help us to be genuinely present where we are.[8]

My children grow tired of being stuck at home, too, and illness-induced cabin fever makes them do strange things. Often their behavior actually worsens as they start to feel better, compared to when they were really sick.

Our children's early bout with a serious upper respiratory virus required them to have daily breathing treatments. For maximum effect, they had to sit still with a mask on during the treatments, and we all know how much one and two year olds love sitting still! Sibling rivalry was rampant during this time, so even though they disliked the treatments, one didn't want the other to get the upper hand. Before each treatment an argument would ensue over who would go first, complete with pushing and shoving. I marveled at the ridiculousness of the situation—fighting to be the first one to do something you hate to do!

Unfortunately, when they're ill, kids have to do all kinds of things they dislike. Number one on our children's list is taking medicine. I've often thought our priorities as a society are a bit off; we can send men to the moon, but we can't seem to make a medicine that children enjoy taking! I wish it could be as simple as in the song from Mary Poppins, "Just a spoonful of sugar helps the medicine go down. . . ." Here are some tips, collected from our various pediatricians, on how to help the medicine go down. We had to try several of these techniques before we found the one that worked best for each medicine and each child.

Placement is everything. Reduce the chances of your

baby spitting out medicine by placing it in the side of the mouth, between cheek and gum. This way you'll avoid as many taste buds as possible.

Cool it down. Some medicines taste better when cold. Ask your pharmacist if your child's prescription can be chilled.

Try a different flavor. The same medicine may come in a variety of flavors, so try to accommodate your child's preferences.

Mix with something yummy. Mary Poppins was right! Try mixing medicine in a spoonful of applesauce, jam, or peanut butter, or offer a drink of milk, formula, or juice to wash the medicine down. (Check with your pharmacist first. The interaction of some food and drugs can make the medicine less effective.)

Another thing our children practiced, sick and healthy, was washing their hands. One naturally enjoyed playing in the water. The others were coaxed into washing their hands with a couple of fun gimmicks. First, I filled an empty "honey bear" plastic honey bottle with liquid soap to make washing a treat. To ensure they did more than wave their hands under the faucet, we rubbed our soapy hands together until we'd sung one entire verse of the ABC song (helps with learning letters, too). A preschool teacher taught my son this germ warfare tactic. Instead of having kids sneeze or cough into their hands, and then proceed to touch everything in sight depositing germs along the way, ask them to bend their arm and sneeze or cough into the "V" made at the elbow.

No matter how many precautions we took, at some point in a child's illness I'd begin to wonder when the other shoe was going to drop. When would the next child come down with it? When would I? Inevitably, there were times when I came down with the latest bug, too. As a mom I know says, "The only thing worse than having sick kids at home is being sick yourself with healthy kids at home."

My friend, Mary, tells of a time when her entire family was stricken with food poisoning. Her husband was lying on the couch, a couple of kids were scattered about the floor, and she was leaning over the toilet with her two-year-old daughter pulling on her hair. It's hard to get any sympathy, much less help, when you're the one on the sick bed. But don't overlook the healing power of prayer. In his psalms, David reminds us of God's unfailing attention to our needs: "They cried out to the Lord in their trouble, and he brought them out of their distress" (Psalm 107:28).

Moms also need practical survival tactics to get through those days when they're down for the count. Pull out sleeping bags (if you have them), or lay a big blanket on the floor to make a play space. This makes it easier to keep track of your kids while they play and watch videos—and you crash on the couch. Call and have lunch or dinner delivered so you don't have to get everyone dressed and out of the house. If you have a toddler, let her play with crayons and paper or

Play-Doh while sitting in her highchair. Use the time to enjoy a cup of herbal tea.

"A cheerful heart is good medicine" (Proverbs 17:22). A useful tool for cheering up sick children (or healthy ones with sick moms) is a Sick Day Survival Box. Keep a sturdy plastic box on hand filled with Happy Meal toys, small cars, plastic figurines, paper and colored pencils, simple puzzles, picture books, stories and music on cassette tapes or CDs, small stuffed animals, puppets, funny hats, and other treasures. Keep the box stashed away to bring out only when your child needs to play quietly. Add new surprises to the box from time to time.

Having sick children can be scary and reassurance that our child will be healed can sometimes be hard to find. Our first pediatrician was a compassionate man who, incidentally, had children exactly the same ages as ours. He also had the unfortunate habit of always presenting us with the worst case scenario. Being well-informed about all aspects of your children's health is very important, but when they were very young, we looked to our pediatrician for reassurance as much as information.

Our children look to us to help them feel better, but where can a mom turn for comfort? It's tempting to play "Let's Make a Deal" with God when the outcome of an illness or injury is unclear. So tempting, in fact, that we forget to be grateful that He is already right there with us—ready to hear our worries and calm our fears. "As a mother comforts her child, so will I comfort you" (Isaiah 66:13). An illness in the family can bring a mom to her knees faster than just about anything—instinctively we reach for the Lord in our time of need.

The New Testament contains many stories of Jesus healing the sick. In each instance, Jesus acts as the instrument of healing, but it is through faith that the sick become whole again.

> *When Jesus had entered Capernaum, a centurion came to him, asking for help. "Lord," he said, "my servant lies at home paralyzed and in terrible suffering." Jesus said to him, "I will go and heal him." The centurion replied, "Lord, I do not deserve to have you come under my roof. But just say the word, and my servant will be healed." . . . When Jesus heard this, he was astonished and said to those following him, "I tell you the truth, I have not found anyone in Israel with such great faith." . . . Then Jesus said to the centurion, "Go! It will be done just as you believed it would." (Matthew 8:5–13)*

I am not one who is particularly good at being "patient in affliction." But with faith, there is always light at the end of the tunnel—even if we are not yet able to see it. "Peace I leave with you; my peace I give you. I do not give to you as the world gives. Do not let your hearts be troubled and do not be afraid." (John 14:27) The comfort God gives is real and present, without caveats and complications. He does not offer rest for our soul in one hand, and the worst case scenario in the other. With his peace we can be patient and hopeful, in sickness and in health.

Mom's Moments

Keep yourself as healthy as possible by eating a balanced diet, getting some exercise regularly, and taking a multi-vitamin to cover any dietary deficiencies.

Have you put together your Sick Day Survival box yet? Don't forget to keep some of your own favorite cold medicine and pain reliever on hand, so the medicine cabinet won't be bare if you get sick. (Keep all medicines out of the reach of little ones.)

There are many reasons to pray over your children when they are young, but perhaps one of the most tangible prayers is for good health. When you slip into their rooms to check on them before going to bed, say a simple prayer for healing, or for continued good health, like this one patterned after Psalm 109:21: "O Sovereign Lord, deal well with [child's name] for your name's sake; out of the goodness of your love, [heal and] deliver [child's name]."

Role Models Are More than Action Figures

Train a child in the way he should go,
and when he is old he will not turn from it.

PROVERBS 22:6

Let's play a word association game. When I say the phrase "role model," what comes first to mind? I usually think of role models in relation to older kids, as in "My sister's excellent academic record encouraged me to work hard for good grades." But young children are every bit in need of positive role models in their lives. Although they come into this world with some characteristics already set, in many ways babies are still blank slates—waiting for our modeling to mesh with their personality and help create the people they will become.

Friends in the field of education often tell me, "You are your child's first teacher." And me without a teaching certificate! But seriously, how hard can being a role model for a baby or toddler be? Moms naturally model things like love, care, and constancy for their babies and move up to more challenging skills like sharing, cooperation, and forgiveness as their children grow.

I remember once eavesdropping on a somewhat unusual playtime. My oldest son was holding some heroic plastic action figure, my daughter a Barbie doll, and my youngest son a stuffed teddy bear. Somehow they had managed to integrate all three wildly different toys into a story line—and they were getting along!

Spencer said something like, "Pretend Captain Superhero uncovered a plot to destroy the universe." Shelby answered, "And say Detective Barbie uses her tools to find the identity of the evildoers." And Ross chimed in, "And then Teddy drives his Tonka tow truck in to save the day!"

It's times like these I feel that I've gotten "it" right. What is "it?" Teaching my kids some important life skill. They didn't learn the powers of negotiation and compromise from inanimate toys, though no doubt they have honed those skills by practicing on each other. I have to believe that some of their ability to work together is a result of the many times we sat and discussed how to "play nicely," as well as the modeling I demonstrated when we pretended together. (At least I really hope so!)

While it's nice to congratulate myself for those times my training has gone right, there are also instances when my example hasn't taken hold. For example, why is my son the only preschooler in the entire congregation who can't seem to remember not to pick his nose while sitting at the front of the church during children's story time? There's also the fact that some of those skills I mentioned are a little harder to model than I thought.

Take sharing. Even though it's one of the first skills we encourage in our children, sharing can be a difficult skill for moms to practice. We already share so much: our resources, our time, even our bodies. When my kids first started looking at the food on my plate and saying "I try," I was thrilled to introduce them to new taste sensations. But things quickly got out of control. Trying to discreetly enjoy the last can of my favorite diet soft drink, I'd hear, "Sip?" I seemed to be the only one doing any sharing. When I asked for a bite of their ice cream, the answer was always "no." The last straw came when one of them caught me sneaking a piece of gourmet chocolate I'd received for Valentine's Day. "Bite?" That time I said "no."

Then there's cooperation—it's really so much faster and easier to get things done if I do them myself, without my children's "help." Baking and decorating cookies, a forty-five minute job on my own, turns into a two hour marathon when we work together—and that's not including clean-up, which no one offers to help with. Modeling cooperation with young children usually means accepting more of a mess and relaxing your standards so that you can enjoy the feeling of accomplishment together.

Demonstrate forgiveness? Sure, my kids should forgive the child who grabs a toy from their hands. But that lamp they broke was the last thing given to me by my grandmother before she passed away (as well as the only remaining piece of glass in the house)! Forgiveness is almost always near the top on the list of qualities we'd like to impart. But adults often exhibit a prideful bias against having to forgive children, or we simply overlook the need to give and ask for pardon from those so young. Moms must be intentional in putting forth the time and effort to say "I'm sorry" or "I forgive you" to model forgiveness.

The quality I have the most trouble with is constancy. How many times have I said I'd play with or read to my child "in a minute," but then get busy with something else? Young children tend to categorize any such statement as a promise. Am I standing on my promises? My reneging is not intentional, but if values are more often caught than taught, I worry *what are my kids "catching" from me?* Watching their occasional full-blown, lying-on-the-floor, kicking-and-screaming-'till-their-face-turns-blue tantrum gives me pause—I wonder what my own adult outbursts look like to them.

Another principle I have tried to impart to my kids is peaceableness. When they began showing an interest in watching TV, I gave up tuning in to the evening news. I felt the disturbing and violent images were not appropriate for their impressionable minds. With our first son we banished weapons like toy guns and swords from the toy box. Imagine my surprise when he began transforming his Tinkertoys, sticks, and even his fingers into weapons. My first attempt at modeling non-violence—the "pretend it doesn't exist and hope they don't notice" approach—was not a complete success. This experience taught me that being a role model is not a one shot deal, but a process. If one approach doesn't work, you have to try another—like spending lots of time talking about why physically hurting others is a bad thing.

Sometimes being a role model yields unexpected results. One summer our young boys discovered bugs, ants in particular, and felt that any poor ant crawling across the sidewalk was just begging to be stepped on, so we spent a lot of time talking about love and respect for all living things. Later that summer my father took us all fishing for the first time. (Fishing was a hobby of ours while I was growing up.) On this particular trip the only "keeper" was caught by my oldest son, who promptly cried until we agreed to release it. He was filled with compassion over the plight of the fish. I thought we might have to take my father, the sports fisherman, to the hospital for stitches—he was biting his lip so hard. I imagine my dad felt this was one lesson learned a little too well!

My friend Tina related a similar experience: "My niece's preschool class took a field trip to a turkey farm before Thanksgiving. When my father opened the oven door on Thanksgiving Day and pulled the turkey out, she burst into tears. My mom fixed her a grilled cheese sandwich instead. What could she do? My niece was five, she went to see the live turkeys, and two days later we were eating one! She couldn't handle it."

In raising children, the time horizon between "training" them, and actually seeing results, can be long enough that we begin to despair of our efforts. Do you think Jesus ever became discouraged by the disciples' occasional lack of "catching on" to the example he provided? Even on the night of their last meal together he modeled a simple act of humility and servitude and encouraged them to do the same.

> When he had finished washing their feet, he put on his clothes and returned to his place. "Do you understand what I have done for you?" he asked them. "You call me 'Teacher' and 'Lord,' and rightly so, for that is what I am. Now that I, your Lord and Teacher, have washed your feet, you also should wash one another's feet. I have set you an example that you should do as I have done for you." (John 13:12–15)

I've had moments when a child has clearly "caught" some positive training, but there have also been times when I've heard my daughter nagging her brothers and thought, "Do I sound like that?" It's not so pleasant to hear those unflattering things and know that you've modeled those, too. Is any other mother intimidated by the fact that there are little eyes and ears constantly absorbing whatever we do? I guess I feel pressured because I know that I am not the perfect role model. That fact has become apparent to me on many levels—not the least of which is my children's propensity toward pointing out my mistakes.

Take, for instance, a recent telemarketer's phone call. We can receive four or more of these calls on a daily basis, which can be aggravating, to say the least. I had heard a woman mention that she quickly dispatched callers asking for her husband by telling them, "He doesn't live here anymore," so I decided to try out this technique on the next sales call. Unfortunately, my son was standing nearby. Our ensuing conversation went something like this:

Spencer: "Are we moving somewhere else?"

Me: "Not that I know of."

Spencer: "Is daddy moving away?"

Me: "No!"

Spencer (tearfully): "Are you getting a divorce?"

Me: "Of course not. Why would you ask such a thing?"

Spencer: "Well, you just told that person on the phone that Daddy doesn't live here anymore."

Me: "I was just trying to get off the phone quickly."

Spencer: "Oh, so you lied?"

"In everything set them an example by doing what is good. In your teaching show integrity, seriousness and soundness of speech that cannot be condemned" (Titus 2:7–8). Oops! One "innocent" falsehood certainly opened a big can of worms. Do you ever feel as if the Lord gave you children in order to point out areas in your life where work is needed? Thinking about what comes out of my mouth *before* I say it would qualify as an "under construction" area for me.

Being a role model is stressful. I can understand why some sports icons have said they don't want the job. One little slip and you're spending ten minutes explaining to your child why they should do as you say and not necessarily as you do. Those toy role models have it easy! I wish I could do every job as perfectly as Barbie (and look good, too). It helps to realize that I am growing into this role as a model for my children. Perhaps the first precept to remember in becoming a role model is the Golden Rule. We should act toward others as we would like them to act towards us. By demonstrating sharing, cooperation, forgiveness, constancy, peaceableness, and honesty in our interactions, I hope my children will internalize those same qualities.

Obviously, we cannot always set perfect examples for our children—God is the only perfect parent. But kids can learn from the things we do wrong, as well as from the things we do right. They can watch us make a mistake, see that it's not fatal, and observe as we correct it. They can hear us get angry at their actions, then regain our composure and say, "That's okay. I love you." The gift of motherhood should motivate us to continue growing in new and better ways, and our children get to watch and be a part of that process, too. I know that I am an imperfect example, but as the person my preschoolers look up to most in the world, I also know how important it is to keep trying.

Even when we do things right, others can incorrectly interpret our words and actions. In this childhood story from my friend Kathy, her little brother's remarks cast some doubt, in a hilarious way, about their mother's suitability as a role model:

My dad was a state policeman, and he worked all different hours. One day, when my brother was about three years old, my dad came home in his uniform and parked his squad car in the driveway. My father's stepmother was visiting at the time, and when dad arrived my mom said, "Oh, Wendell's home." So my brother echoed, "Oh, good, Wendell's here." My father's stepmother, not thinking that a child would refer to his father by his given name, asked, "Who's Wendell?" My brother replied, "He's a guy that's a good friend of my mom's." For some reason, my brother thought the guy in the uniform was a different person than my dad. My mom was mortified!

Talk to any mom and you'll find she probably has at least one child that humbles her on a regular basis. I have a child like that. One day at his Christian preschool my son actually stood on a chair, for maximum effect, and clearly pronounced a new word he had learned. Unfortunately, it was not the kind of word that should be coming from the mouth of a four year old. Immediately, every head whipped in my direction. My mind raced from considering where the choice word had been heard to trying to find that proverbial "hole in the ground" to crawl into. It was not our finest moment.

But not all moments of humility are negative. This same child informed me one day, while I was ranting and raving in a particularly bad mood, that I "was not being very nice" and should "think to myself, 'What would Jesus do?' in this situation." Hold the phone! Was a child leading me to appropriate behavior?

By focusing on my role as teacher—stacking up blocks so they don't fall down, getting clothes on right side out—I sometimes overlook that God brought children into my life to teach me things, too. "Don't let anyone look down on you because you are young, but set an example for the believers in speech, in life, in love, in faith and in purity" (1 Timothy 4:12). How important it is to be open to those gentle messages God sends through young role models, my children, and to celebrate and encourage their ability to be positive examples for others.

"You are the light of the world. A city on a hill cannot be hidden. Neither do people light a lamp and put it under a bowl. Instead they put it on its stand, and it gives light to everyone in the house. In the same way, let your light shine before men, that they may see your good deeds and praise your

Father in heaven" (Matthew 5:14–16). We represent God's "light" to our children. Many of us have events or deeds in our past that make us uncertain of our suitability to be a role model. But with our kids, as with the Lord, we start with a clean slate. Don't allow guilt and self-doubt to hide your light. Our children only see the example set before them today. By following the Lord's model in "training a child in the way he should go," you lay a foundation that kids can return to as they grow and other potential role models enter their lives.

Mom's Moments

Is there one area of your life where you could set a better example for your family—in action, speech, love, or faith?

Perhaps you need a break from being a role model. Taking some time off with another mom temporarily removes you from that role and gives you the opportunity to share your challenges with someone who's also "in the trenches."

Think about role models in your life. How did they positively affect you, even with their own imperfections?

Gravity and Other Forces of Nature

The Lord does not look at the things man looks at.
Man looks at the outward appearance,
but the Lord looks at the heart.

1 SAMUEL 16:7

One day my daughter and I were driving through town. I was reading all the signs on the buildings out loud for her. We drove by an automotive repair establishment and I read, "Body Shop." My daughter asked, "Is that where people get tattoos and stuff?" (I was afraid to ask what other "stuff" she was referring to.) "No," I replied, "it's for collision repair for cars when they've had an accident." Do you ever feel like your body and motherhood have collided? We know that motherhood changes our heart, but the sum of the equation "any number of pregnancies plus natural aging" can result in some unexpected modifications in our appearance, too.

Coming to terms with the physical changes of motherhood is not always easy. I harbored the misconception that my body would snap back into shape like a rubber band once my baby was born. Some first-time moms I know brought their old pre-pregnancy jeans with them to wear home from the hospital. To their credit, a few of them actually could fit into those jeans. (Okay, maybe one.)

I didn't have my first child until age thirty, and my body definitely didn't bounce back into shape as I hoped. Imagine a rubber band wrapped around a large stack of paper for an extended period of time, say nine months. The elasticity tends to decline, so that when the band is finally unwrapped, it's just a stretched out version of its former self. That was me.

Lots of us struggle to regain our shape after a baby arrives. A friend of mine shared this story about her sister-in-law that illustrates a new mom's battle with the bulge.

My husband's sister had a little trouble losing weight after the birth of her second child. When her new daughter was four months old, she and I were both invited to her sister's fortieth birthday party, so she wore one of her maternity dresses because that was all that was comfortable at the time. While we were mingling at the party, a woman came up to her and said,

"Congratulations! When. . ." My sister-in-law knew the woman was going to ask her when the baby was due, so she cut her off and said, "Oh, thank you so much. She's four months already!" I've always thought that was such a classy answer to an embarrassing situation.

I, too, have been asked if I was pregnant when I wasn't. But my "baby" was over a year old. I was still wearing one of my "smarter" maternity outfits. Maternity clothes do look so much better than in my own mother's time! And I had a tendency to avoid buying new postpartum clothes until I got back to my ideal weight. Unfortunately, I've never really gotten back to it.

Now more than ever I agree with this sentiment expressed by humorist Erma Bombeck, "I never leaf through a copy of *National Geographic* without realizing how lucky we are to live in a society where it is traditional to wear clothes." How many different sized clothes do you have in your closet? Most moms have at least two: "thin" clothes and "regular." Someone once jokingly told me that when we get our new bodies in heaven, our new dress size will be determined according to the Scripture verse, "many who are first will be last, and many who are last will be first" (Matthew 19:30). Meaning if you wear a larger size now, you'll flip-flop to a size 6. This works for me!

Jesus gives this statement in regard to loving our enemies: "Be perfect, therefore, as your heavenly Father is perfect" (Matthew 5:48). How often we consider our own bodies the enemy! Christ sets up the high ideal of perfection in love and spirit, not in appearance. But what about the Madison Avenue standard for looks or the Paris fashion show standard?

My body now looks much more like a Botticelli painting than an advertisement in a fashion magazine. The book of Proverbs gives this warning to men against seductresses, but it serves equally well for women who are seduced by the pursuit of beauty: "Do not lust in your heart after her beauty or let her captivate you with her eyes" (Proverbs 6:25). With the parade of young, beautiful girls the media constantly sets before us as examples of the ideal woman, it's hard not to be captivated—as well as convinced to buy the latest anti-cellulite cream, push-up bra, or under-eye concealer.

Of course other changes come to our bodies that are simply hazards of motherhood and maturity (a.k.a. age). Has anyone else noticed things starting to sag? After breast-feeding three babies, I can no longer pass the pencil test. Let me go back a bit here—actually way, way back. When I was in high school physical education class (girls only), we spent one semester doing toning exercises. As body conscious and giggly teens, the chest toning drills had us in stitches. One of the girls taught us all a chant, ostensibly to make the exercises pass more quickly. "We must, we must, we must increase our bust." I'm sure you get the idea.

Our P. E. teacher told us these exercises would help keep certain parts of our anatomy from sagging. She then encouraged us to try the pencil test at home to gauge our progress.

To take the test, you place a pencil underneath your breast, and if the pencil falls to the ground by itself, there's no sagging. (However, I suspect cup size has as much to do with whether you pass the test as how well-toned you are.) It's depressing to realize that I have become the very thing I feared in high school.

That's probably more than you needed to know about my anatomy, but I wanted to get it out there to illustrate the point that things change after you have children. For many of us, the most striking and lasting changes are the physical ones. Thankfully, some of these changes, though just as permanent as the one I previously discussed, are at least "fixable" without surgery.

As did my mother, I began to notice the appearance of stray gray hairs in my late twenties. But by the time I was thirty-six, and eight-and-a-half-months pregnant with my third child, the gray was impossible to miss. I went to my hairdresser for one last trim before my baby arrived, and while there, we consulted about putting some highlights in to cover the gray. (By the way, I did earn every one of those gray hairs that came in while raising my first two kids!)

I should explain here that we live in a rural farming community with a population of about eleven hundred. Couples here tend to start their families at a younger age, so I was something of an oddity. In fact, an older patron in the beauty shop very tactfully asked, "Well, how old are you, anyway?" When I told her I was thirty-six she replied, "You could be a grandmother!" Let me tell you, that made my day. NOT! Thank goodness hair color is one physical change that's easy to fix.

Even though we tend to keep a running tally of each new bulge and complexion flaw, young children often don't relate body size or physical imperfections to those in their own families. For example, they may refer to someone on the street as "fat" (and be gently corrected), but it would not occur to them to use that same label on a family member they have come to know and love. "Parents are the pride of their children" (Proverbs 17:6). And indeed we are, whatever we look like. In our kids' eyes we catch a glimpse of agape love—the limitless, unconditional love that only God can truly give. They do not judge us based on appearance, but rather on our importance in their lives.

Wouldn't it be wonderful if we could recapture some of that childlike acceptance of our own bodies? Jesus said, "I tell you the truth, unless you change and become like little children, you will never enter the kingdom of heaven" (Matthew 18:3). Having a poor body image will not in and of itself exclude us from God's kingdom. But with all the not-so-subtle media messages we receive about appearance, we must take care not to set body image up as an idol to be worshiped.

So how can a mom learn to embrace the way she looks? Here is a seven step plan to help move from body self-consciousness toward acceptance of the real you, outside and in.

1. Realize that coming to terms with your body is a lifelong process. If you've had a baby recently, your body has undergone tremendous changes. However, everyone's body is in a constant state of change, so there's always something new to embrace. Do your best to let go of how you "used to look" and accept your current attributes.

2. Get real! How many average-looking women do you see represented in popular media? In soap operas and so-called reality TV shows the women are all buff, beautiful, and (dare I say it?) usually blond. Where are moms with spit-up on their shoulders? Where are the women who don't have Barbie-esque dimensions, and don't aspire to? Don't fall into the trap of having your "reality" dictated to you by what you see on billboards, in magazines, and on TV. Instead, follow the real advice of Proverbs 31:30, "Charm is deceptive, and beauty is fleeting; but a woman who fears the Lord is to be praised."

3. Stop comparison shopping. If you have a picture in your head of the perfect-looking mom, that image is almost always a composite of things you like about a variety of women. No one person is perfect, so how can you expect yourself to match up against such an unrealistic ideal? Comparisons we make between ourselves and others are usually unfavorable on our end and give us an unfairly negative

image of ourselves. "Accept one another, then, just as Christ accepted you, in order to bring praise to God" (Romans 15:7). We need to be as accepting of ourselves as we are willing to be of others.

4. Put your best foot forward. Pick out one or two or three of your best features and emphasize them. Everyone can find something to like about themselves. Perhaps you have good feet—get a pedicure and a pair of cute sandals. Maybe your eyes are your best feature. Stop by a cosmetics counter (alone) and ask the salesperson to show you the newest makeup to bring them out. If you have good posture, make an appointment for a massage to get the kinks out.

5. Change your measuring stick. If you've been basing your idea of body image solely on appearance, it's time for a new frame of reference. Consider your body in terms of health instead of just beauty. Healthy does not necessarily mean thin. "The discerning heart seeks knowledge, but the mouth of a fool feeds on folly" (Proverbs 15:14). (Or in my case, Cheese Curls and Oreos.) Educate yourself about food choices. There is a wealth of nutritional information out there today, but sometimes it seems to conflict itself. Today's best dietary weapon against cancer is tomorrow's suspected carcinogen. My grandmother, who grew up during a time when food was less processed and less varied, has

lived a healthful ninety-eight years by sticking to the motto, "Everything in moderation."

6. Exercise—just do it! You knew the "E" word was going to crop up sooner or later. Besides helping with weight loss and improving your cardiovascular system, exercise is one of the best things you can do to counteract the negative effects of stress on your body. If it's been awhile since your exercise program included more than picking up baby, here are some tips on how to get started. First, pick an exercise activity that you enjoy—you'll be more likely to keep it up over time. Walking is still one of the most recommended activities for new exercisers, but there are loads of fun workout videos and DVDs available so you can exercise inside as well. Second, don't try to do too much too soon. Overexertion and sore body parts often lead to the novice exerciser's main enemy: burnout. Start out with 10–20 minutes the first week, and increase your exercise time slowly. Finally, the secret to consistently sticking with a long-term exercise plan is variety. Incorporating different kinds of exercises into your routine keep your mind and your body from getting bored.

Whatever our shape, it's easier to accept if we feel healthy and strong. Scripture provides beautiful imagery of a healthy body, which is actually a description of how we grow together in Christ:

"From Him the whole body, joined and held together by every supporting ligament, grows and builds itself up in love, as each part does its work" (Ephesians 4:16). As we work each part of our body, we find ourselves growing in strength and support.

7. How you look is not who you are. Remind yourself that how you look is not the most important thing about you. "Your beauty should not come from outward adornment, such as braided hair and the wearing of gold jewelry and fine clothes. Instead, it should be that of your inner self, the unfading beauty of a gentle and quiet spirit, which is of great worth in God's sight" (1 Peter 3:3–4). Clearly it is even more important to work on your inner beauty. A growing relationship with the Lord will never sag or develop wrinkles. No physical changes will separate us from the love of God (see Romans 8:39). Drawing closer to Him is one regimen that will always yield results.

Now that I've laid out the reasons a healthy body image is important, I have a confession to make. None of them were the real motivators for wrestling with my own body consciousness. It took a close friend's eating disorder and comments about dieting from my preschool daughter to give me a wake-up call about the way my own body image was affecting my family.

I'm not very good at dieting, but that hasn't stopped

my trying it from time to time. Of course, my children carefully watched what I ate or didn't eat (sometimes more carefully than I did). "Why aren't you having dinner, Mommy?" "Why is Mommy eating special food?" It became increasingly difficult to explain away the restrictions or unusual requirements of the latest fad diet I was trying (the grapefruit diet, one-meal-a-day diet, high-protein diet, and so on).

My bad habits were causing my children to internalize negative messages about food instead of learning to appreciate different foods and how eating them nourishes our bodies. Even worse, my kids started looking at their own bodies with a critical eye. I realized that if I was really serious about helping them look at a person's heart instead of their appearance, as God does, then I had to live out that belief, not just give it lip service.

Turning our focus from "outside" to "inside" takes more than concentrating on a healthy body instead of a thin one. Kids need balance in the messages they receive from us to understand that good looks do not guarantee "goodness" in a person's heart (and vice versa). Children are bound to eventually ask, "How do I look?" We can tell them how beautiful they are and compliment a positive character quality, like patience they showed with a younger sibling or having a pleasant attitude. Each of us is a special creation designed by God. Recognizing our good qualities on the inside and the outside helps us deal with whatever changes time and life may bring.

Mom's Moments

If you are having trouble starting or sticking to a dietary or exercise program, copy and post this Bible verse around the house for encouragement: "I can do everything through him who gives me strength" (Philippians 4:13).

Eleanor Roosevelt said, "No one can make you feel inferior without your consent." If you are particularly susceptible to unrealistic portrayals of body image in the media, exercise your right to turn off the TV or discontinue a magazine subscription.

Work on that inner beauty by giving yourself a soul makeover. Keep your Bible in the bathroom to read a couple verses whenever you can steal a few minutes. Find a book of God's promises or other inspirational quotes that affirm His love and care for you.

I Love You, You Love Me

A friend loves at all times.

PROVERBS 17:17

Whenhen it comes to friendships, moms with young children are faced with a dilemma. They need loving, supportive relationships more than ever, but maintaining them becomes much more of a challenge when children are added into the mix. Even as my relationship with each of my children bloomed, my other "adult" relationships seemed to wither or, at the very least, lose their spark.

Our desire for meaningful connections with others is described by author Sharon Hersh in her book *Bravehearts*. "Deep within every woman is a heart full of longing for relationships. It is a longing that whispers, 'Ask me, notice me, hear me, know me, understand me, believe me, enjoy me, stay with me, care for me—and receive all of these from me as well.' We long to meet other's needs and get our own needs met. This possibility of loving and being loved extravagantly ignites a spark in every woman's heart." [9]

Becoming a mother changes us, and as much as we may wish otherwise, it often changes the ways we relate to those close to us. As our time and attention are poured into a new life, our friendships become disjointed—even neglected. While God is our most enduring and ever-present friend, He designed people, especially women, to live in community with others. A close relationship with Him is not a substitute for face-to-face interaction; sometimes only togetherness with other human beings soothes our longing to feel connected.

Scripture provides us with many examples of the importance of friendship. One of the most beautiful relationships is that of David and Jonathan from 1 Samuel 18-20. Jonathan expressed his heartfelt love and friendship for David by protecting him from the jealous and murderous intentions of Jonathan's father, Saul (that's King Saul to you and me). Jonathan truly acted as a lifeline to David, even to the point of defying his father. The depth of feeling between them was such that, when David had to quickly leave town, "they kissed each other and wept together—but David wept the most" (1 Samuel 20:41).

Jesus considered His disciples friends rather than servants.

His love for them was so great that He wanted them to extend that feeling to each other. "A new command I give you: Love one another. As I have loved you, so you must love one another" (John 13:34). Moms need, long for, and are designed to enjoy loving relationships. But how can we follow Christ's command in our relationships with other adults when caring for our children takes up so much of our time and energy? Is it possible to maintain and even deepen our friendships during this busy season?

One of the most difficult friendship transitions occurs between new moms and women without children. Other women in the trenches of motherhood understand the necessity of attending to a young child's constant needs. They tend to make allowances for our frequent inability to finish a coherent sentence or to remember to ask what's new in their lives.

Women without children do not share the same experience. While our lives as women have changed dramatically and permanently, theirs may have continued on pretty much as before. Obviously, some friction may result as each of us struggles to find a new equilibrium together. In order to gain perspective from the other side of the friendship circle, I asked a single friend to explain the differences she has noticed in her relationships with new moms.

When a friend has a new baby, her life changes to revolve around her child. From my standpoint, a new mom appears to lose herself as a person—the focus of any conversation and activity is on her baby. Going out together

*is a completely different experience. I feel like we're
always hurrying and trying to keep the baby entertained.*

*I get annoyed with the child, because I want to spend
time with my friend and the baby keeps interrupting. I
get annoyed with my friend, because it's hard for her to
be completely present when we talk—her attention is
always being diverted elsewhere. The ultimate impact
on our relationship is that I feel a bit resentful and don't
want to spend as much time together.*

If this type of a friendship is important enough to maintain, concessions have to be made for the long-term on both sides. According to marriage and family therapist Leslie Parrott, "Friends help us move beyond mommyhood to maintain an adult perspective on living." Women not immediately focused on child rearing are particularly good at helping us think "outside the box," or at least beyond the home front. As moms, we have had the opportunity to live in both worlds, with children and without. Try to remember the things you and your friend enjoyed talking about and doing together before kids, and make arrangements to spend time alone (or at least while your child naps) so you can share some undivided attention. You may not see each other as often, but the time you spend together can at least be quality time.

Friendships with other women who are moms can also fall by the wayside. These breaks can be due to several factors: different family ages and stages, conflicting mothering styles, and personality differences between children. Before my first child was born, I enjoyed the company of a group of moms whose children were in the late preschool to early elementary age range—old enough to make it easier for their moms to get out and do things together. I joined the bowling league, took day-trips, and went shopping with my new-found friends. After my son arrived, they dutifully came to visit and wish us well. But from then on, I saw them only rarely. They had moved beyond the restrictions of frequent naps, feedings, and changings. Since their kids were all about the same age, they could play together without fear of serious injury, or at least without constant supervision. The ages of our children and the differences in our families' developmental stages made it difficult to maintain our friendship.

Conflicting mothering styles can be another impediment to friendship. Mellow. Type A. Hands-on. Detached. The very traits that attract you to a person in friendship tend to push you apart when they result in different approaches to mothering. I've mentioned that I was rather uptight with our first child—sometimes with good reason. He was the type of baby who, although breast-fed and able to spend most of his days in his own relatively germ-free home, mysteriously contracted every illness possible.

A sick, fussy baby was bad enough. But for this baby, virtually every illness guaranteed a trip to the pediatrician. Never mind the number of hours we spent in the doctor's waiting room, the medical costs were staggering! Needless to say, after several months of almost weekly visits to the clinic, we began to avoid circumstances where he could catch yet another bug.

Illnesses were not such a big deal to other moms. (I referred to them as "mellow moms.") Either their kids had more active immune systems or they simply handled a fever-ish baby more calmly than I. My own experience led me to be overly cautious about exposing other children when my son was sick. A mellow mom's attitude would be: "What's the big deal? It's just a runny nose." One mom in my first playgroup was like that. She arrived each week with her two preschool-ers in tow whether they were healthy or not. The only time she missed playgroup was when she herself was too sick to attend. I raged to myself about her lack of decorum—and tried to keep her children's toys out of my child's mouth. Our differ-ing approaches toward child rearing made it difficult for a friendship to blossom beyond our weekly playgroup meetings.

A simple case of personality opposites in kids shouldn't interfere with a friendship between moms, right? I mean, our children shouldn't dictate our choice of friends. Easier said than done. One of my closest friends during the preschool years was the mother of a prim and proper little girl while I had a little "Bam-Bam." My son was a typically boisterous, often clueless boy. Talk about your Venus and Mars! Our kids had nothing in common, unless you count the mutual dislike they harbored toward one another.

Her daughter would sometimes tease (terrorize) my son until he lashed out in typical Bam-Bam style. You know how it is—the one who retaliates is often the one who gets caught and is ultimately punished. And my son spent an inordinate amount of each visit in time-outs. I finally did a bit of spying on their playtime to see for myself what could prompt my physical son to abandon pounding on the workbench in favor of pounding on my friend's daughter.

Catching the precocious little girl in the act helped me understand my son's behavior, but it did not improve my attitude toward my friend. In fact, despite several conversations between us in an attempt to analyze why our children couldn't get along, it wasn't until she had a boy of her own (and I a girl) that we could both say, "Now I know what you were talking about!" Our friendship stood the test of time and kids who are opposites, but it wasn't always easy.

Given all the difficulties in developing and maintaining friendships in this season of life, you may be tempted to withdraw or even question the very need for close relationships. So why does a busy mom need friendships? Because friends enrich our lives, friends help us become better moms, and good friends help us when we need it most.

Two are better than one. . .if one falls down, his friend can help him up. But pity the man who falls and has no one to help him up! (Ecclesiastes 4:9–10)

Part of the solution to the puzzle of making and keeping friends when you have young children is the realization that adult relationships come in all shapes and sizes. We are not bound by the "one best friend" constraint to which kids often feel tied. Proverbs 17:17 tells us that, "A friend loves at all times." It does not say that all the love we require can come from one friend. With the complexity of our lives, no one person can meet all of our needs for empathy, support, and companionship—nor should we expect them to.

It's perfectly natural to have a friend down the street with whom you share your everyday problems, a friend with older children who you turn to for perspective on the things your kids do, and a friend who has known you forever and loves you even though you haven't seen each other for a few years. An African proverb describes two of these types of people that we often include in our friendship circle: friends of the road, who we meet by chance, and friends of the heart, bound to us by choice.

Most of our friends are friends of the road—those we are thrown together with often who happen to live in close proximity: neighbors, co-workers, or women in the groups we attend. They know of our comings and goings. They are part of our everyday lives, and so they would be missed if they were gone. Because our lives are so intertwined, friends of the road will help with a difficult project, watch one child "for a minute" while you grab the other, or lend us that proverbial cup of sugar we often need.

A friend of the heart sees us as a better version of ourselves—just being around her makes us feel as smart, funny, and "together" as we wish we were. She's a confidante, a cheerleader, and sometimes, a partner in crime. Friends of the road can become friends of the heart. But friendships of the heart are harder to find; rarely do they arrive on our doorstep wrapped up in a bow. Developing this type of friendship usually requires us to take some initiative. If friendships of the heart are lacking in your relationships, look for situations like these that put you in contact with others who share a common interest:

- attend a continuing education class in your area of expertise

- volunteer for a cause you are passionate about

- sign up to learn a new skill you've always wanted to try

Remember that while children can be an impediment to friendship, they are also a wonderful introduction. You automatically have a great deal in common with any other woman who is also a mother. Let the bond of motherhood act as a catalyst to develop new relationships and fill in your circle of support.

No discussion of loving friendships would be complete without addressing the closest relationship we enjoy with another human being—that with our mate. Dramatic changes occur between husband and wife once they become mom and dad. The impact, both positive and negative, is felt on many different levels. As my husband observed, "We went from having few issues between us because we were focusing on our own relationship to devoting that energy to learning how to be parents. Even though I loved our baby, sometimes

I felt like we were cheating ourselves." On the flip side, we both agree that raising children has given us the opportunity to work as a team and do something extraordinarily important together. Both the joy and the weight of this responsibility have brought us closer as nothing else could.

Physical and psychological changes that accompany motherhood are immediate and profound. Conversely, in many ways new dads remain much the same as before. The aspect of a couple's relationship where this disparity is most evident is the physical one.

That's right, we're talking about sex. I remember very clearly the day of my first six-week postpartum check-up with my obstetrician. He announced that my recovery was progressing nicely and merrily declared that my husband and I could resume our love life. My first reaction was, "You have got to be kidding!" It was hard to know whether to be happy or disappointed by his pronouncement.

When my husband came home from work that day, his face was shining with anticipation. "So, how'd it go?" he asked eagerly.

I had a split-second of indecision. My remembrance of our son's delivery was still pretty fresh. Ouch! I had to think, should I tell him that we were a "go" for marital relations, or should I stall? I won't elaborate here, except to say that we did manage to add two more children to our family in subsequent years.

While parenthood can bring a couple closer together in some respects, the desire for physical intimacy is not always included in this newfound closeness. Fatigue, financial worries, health concerns, and the fact that you've had little people hanging, holding, or sitting on you for most of the day (and thereby exhausted your quota for physical contact) puts many new parents' love relationship on the back burner.

Passion—feeling that spark and acting on it—is an important component of any committed relationship, for moms and especially for dads. If the spark in your love life is in need of some rekindling, read what three moms had to say about how they keep passion alive in their marriage:

We have a family bed, so unless our son is visiting grandparents, our only passion is each other's snores— although we have been creative lately and discovered that couches and floors are nice when you can't get your child in his own bed.

Keeping passion alive is difficult because of exhaustion and financial stresses. But I am discovering that as much as I need to be touched and held by my husband, he needs to be touched and held by me. When we have the chance, we snuggle on the couch together as we watch TV or read the paper—even if that means I don't finish the laundry I started yesterday! We have started communicating better. If I want more attention or have been missing my husband, I make sure I tell him. He has started doing the same. Sometimes that is all it takes to get the passion started, or at least to remind us that it may have been longer than we thought since we were together.

We keep passion alive by having an 8:00 P.M. bedtime for our kids every night, including weekends, so that we can have some time alone together each day. We always go to bed together. If I have to stay up late to feed the baby, my wonderful husband stays up with me. If he has to be up late for some reason, I always wait for him.

As a mother of three, life is hard, and I am constantly being touched all day by my children, physically and emotionally. My husband and I have a regular date night—even if it's at home after the kids are in bed. There's no pressure to make it perfect, and our date doesn't have to involve sex. We play cards, watch a movie, or look at old pictures. Right now, in this season of my life and marriage, I know that to expect an "on-fire" love life is just not reasonable. With that pressure off, when we do make love, it's really special.

The marriage relationship is supposed to be the primary relationship in the family, because though children come, they eventually will go. In Mark 10:7–9 Jesus says, "For this reason a man will leave his father and mother and be united to his wife, and the two will become one flesh. So they are no longer two, but one. Therefore what God has joined together, let man not separate." Don't allow your relationship to become separated by the stresses of life with young children. As Elisa

Morgan and Carol Kuykendall note in *When Husband and Wife Become Mom and Dad,* "Hope comes in realizing that the chaos you're experiencing in your marriage is perfectly normal. The birth of a child does bring an imbalance to your relationship, but here is the important message: You can regain your sense of balance in your marriage by recognizing this as a normal transitional change and learning how to love your way through this transition." [10] A reality of life with kids is that you rarely will find time for your partner—you have to make it. The most precious, valuable, and important friendship you have is worth the effort.

Mom's Moments

Are your high expectations of relationships keeping you from the deep friendships you desire? Are you able to live up to your own standards?

Remember how you and your husband met and fell in love. Reconnect with those days and feelings by retelling your story often, between yourselves as well as to others.

Apply the five-to-one rule in your relationships with those closest to you: Try to give five compliments or do five favors for each single negative comment or action.

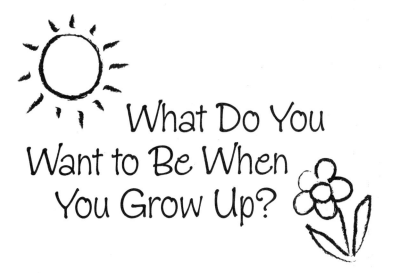

What Do You Want to Be When You Grow Up?

There are different kinds of gifts, but the same Spirit.
There are different kinds of service, but the same Lord.
There are different kinds of working,
but the same God works all of them in all men.

1 CORINTHIANS 12:4–6

Young children have the luxury of "trying on" future professions as they play—sometimes a new one every day. Role playing what they want to be when they grow up is one way for kids to exercise their creative muscle. At different times, my children wanted to be firemen, gymnasts, detectives, doctors, and the President of the United States. Occasionally, their aspirations were not so lofty. One of my sons told me in a single breath that he either wanted to be a scientist or be on Wheel of Fortune.

I asked a couple of other moms to contribute their children's professional preferences:

Kathy: "One of my daughters wanted to be a piano teacher or a plumber."

Cheryl: "My daughter, Ashley, wanted to 'do' hair or be a doctor."

In their innocence, kids are not inhibited by contradictions in their dreams or by the scope of those dreams. Things change as we mature—we become resigned to the thought that there are only one or two things we can do in life. That's why the care and feeding of dreams is so important for children, but it is also important for mothers.

Do you remember what you wanted to "be" when you were a child, a teenager, and a young adult? I attended elementary school during the era when men where landing on the moon, and even though Sally Ride's historic mission as the first woman in space was decades away, I wanted to be an astronaut. My father encouraged this dream of mine by buying me a telescope and staying up weekend nights from 2:00 to 5:00 A.M. trying to catch a glimpse of the elusive planet Saturn. He also spent time looking for canals on the surface of Mars.

As I grew older I developed an interest in photography,

sparked by an old Brownie camera (now an antique) given to me by my grandfather. I became the family archivist on all vacation trips, largely in self-defense. To this day, my parents still cut off the tops of their subjects' heads in photos. I dreamed of living a bohemian lifestyle and taking pictures in exotic locales. After I graduated from college, I wanted to be the youngest female vice president at the bank where I worked. I never really had the opportunity to realize any of those dreams, at least not in the ways I initially envisioned.

So is it necessary for moms to have dreams that extend beyond raising their children? Is it even possible? I believe that it is very important, but not always easy. Sometimes in the process of becoming a mom, the person you were before can disappear right before your eyes. In his letter to the church in Ephesus, Paul writes, "I urge you to live a life worthy of the calling you have received" (Ephesians 4:1). Obviously, we were called to be mothers, but that may not be all we are called to do. We have a responsibility to ourselves, to our families, and to our Lord to use the gifts He gave us to develop something meaningful of our own. You may not have the interest or the energy to launch a new career right now, but you can take baby steps toward fulfilling a lifelong dream. Nurture your creative self and pursue your passion, even with young children at home.

You are pursuing a passion whenever you are creating—whether it's sewing or dancing, cooking or writing, painting or gardening. Why is "creating" important for moms? (By "creating," I mean something different here from "procreating!")

Think about the word "creator." Our original Creator, God, made us in His image. That means we are innately creative, too. We fulfill part of our life's purpose when we express ourselves creatively and pursue a passion. Engaging in a creative endeavor gives moms the opportunity to do something they can feel good about. When I write a phrase that sounds beautiful and is full of expression and meaning, it doesn't matter (as much) that my children were terrors in the grocery store or that they used their safety scissors to cut holes in my new tablecloth. Having some small success at an activity that nurtures my inner creativity means something went "right" that day, regardless of how I feel about the job I've done as Mommy.

We model something wonderful for our children when they see us pursuing a passion—the sense that anything can be possible. Kids see perseverance as they watch us continue on through the ups and downs of a creative activity. Sometimes it turns out the way we hoped, sometimes it doesn't—which is a lot like life. The experience of being a mother is not simply one of giving to others. God designed motherhood to help us learn virtues like selflessness, sacrifice, and patience, but life with children also feeds and nourishes our creative selves. The difficulties inherent in reaching out toward a dream—time, space, and cost—are always overshadowed by the gifts of wonder, laughter, and perspective that our children bring to us.

Still, it can be difficult to break out of the motherhood mold. Kids are creative dynamos! They can figure out how to rotate that other shoulder so they can roll all the way over, devise complicated (and unstable) ways to obtain an object that's out of reach, or use their fingers to smear pudding around their high chair tray in a design that will compete with artwork hung in a museum of modern art. Moms often defer their own creative impulses to those of their children. We place our creativity in a box on a shelf and plan to take it out "when we have more time." Days turn into weeks, months, and years; we wake up one day and feel our creative juices have dried up.

A study of the factors that differentiate creative people from less creative people found that the main distinction was simply this: The creative people thought they were creative, and the less creative people didn't think they were. As a group, mothers with young children are the most creative people I know! Who else but a mother can turn a lump of purple Play-Doh into Barney, come up with 365 ways to stretch a dollar, or simultaneously grate a brick of cheese and read *The Very Hungry Caterpillar* while holding a baby on her lap? But to get those creative juices flowing again, it may be necessary to restate your old dreams in the context of your new life as a mom.

The three things I wanted to be when I grew up—astronaut, photographer, and bank vice president—do have a place in my life. Now I enjoy teaching my children about the constellations and how to tell a planet from a star at night. I'm definitely the family photographer. My husband laughs at our vacation albums and says that when the kids are older they will think just the three of them and my husband went on trips together. I'm literally out of the picture! And wouldn't you know, after "trying on" several careers, my husband found that banking was a good fit. So my six years of banking experience are put to use as a member of the board for the small community bank where he works. "God is able to make all grace abound to you, so that in all things at all times, having all that you need, you will abound in every good work" (2 Corinthians 9:8). God has given me the grace and the opportunity to realize my old dreams in new ways.

Sometimes, however, our dreams become permanently outdated. We all change over time, so it's only natural for our interests to change as well. According to author Roger Von Oech, "Creative thinking is not only constructive, it's also destructive. Often you have to break out of one pattern to discover another one." There are two ways you can go about finding another passion or a new way to express yourself creatively: by purposefully seeking out a new passion or by simply being open to new opportunities as they present themselves.

Try out something new. Picture in your mind what an aerobics instructor looks like. My friend probably doesn't look like the instructor you just imagined. She is a beautiful, strong, fit woman, but she looks a whole lot more like I do than like aerobics video diva Kathy Smith or those ladies from The Firm who star in the exercise videos! Even so, after having her first child she wanted to be healthy and get back in shape, so she started taking classes to become a certified aerobics instructor. It turned out to work well with her life as a mother of preschoolers since the gym where she taught also had child care available (free for instructors). Today she laughs and tells me that's the only way she got a shower during her kids' early years! Because of her willingness to try something new, my friend turned an interest into a hobby, a hobby into a passion, and a passion into a new career.

Open the door when opportunity knocks. You may have noticed that "writer" was not included on my list of what I wanted to be. So how did I get here? About eleven years ago, I met a mom in my first son's playgroup, and she approached me about partnering with her to publish a local newsletter for moms. Her background was in design and advertising, so she asked if I would be willing to write the articles. I had made good grades in English and enjoyed writing, so I said, "Sure." Thank goodness I agreed before taking any time to think about it, and before any of those negative voices in my head started chiming in!

To find your new passion, begin by asking yourself these three questions:

1. If you could do anything with your life, what would it be?

2. When you think back over your childhood, what did you do with your spare time?

3. What would you be if you weren't afraid to fail?

In considering the answers to these questions, a pattern or specific interest may emerge. Once you've identified a passion, or at least a potential one, it's time to start turning your dream into a reality.

The first step is to put together a plan of action. Begin by gathering information—what materials, documents, alterations to your schedule, and child care plans will you need to make? With young children at home, it's important to start small. But don't let this fact keep you from getting started! Remind yourself that each step, no matter how small, is moving you toward your goal. Just like our toddlers, we take baby steps toward it. Revise your action plan as necessary. There may be bumps in the road to pursuing your passion that require changes to your plan. Or you may reach the end of your plan. That's cause for celebration (and a new plan)!

If this seems like more than you would ever be able to achieve, consider what Elisa Morgan and Carol Kuykendall say about why growth can't wait until later in their book, *What Every Mom Needs.*

> *Today represents an important season in your life. You can't skip it or ignore it. And you can't ignore or neglect yourself in this season or you may find a gaping hole in the next. You probably have dreams and desires that need to be expressed. The "you" that has been growing since your own birth doesn't cease to exist because you've given birth to another.*[11]

After putting together a plan, you have to make the time to follow it. With the busyness of this season of our lives, making time can only happen when we know in our hearts that the pursuit of our passion is worthwhile. Have you ever heard the saying, "There's always time for the things that are important to you?" You have to make the expression of your creativity a priority. Put it on the top of your "to do" list at least once a week. And then remember that timing is everything, especially when you have young children. Those baby steps toward your goal need to fit into your family's schedule. You can add on more activities as time and your lifestyle allow.

The final thing needed to follow a dream is persistence. It's easy to say to ourselves, "I'm going to make creative expression a weekly priority." But then the kids get sick and we overextend our schedules; before we know it, a month goes by without accomplishing anything. Beyond the daily or weekly discipline it takes to stick with your interest, you need special persistence to come back to a passion again and again as life intervenes.

There is another way in which persistence pays off: overcoming the fear of failure. If we really look inside ourselves, we may find the biggest roadblock to pursuing our passion isn't time or money, but the possibility that we won't succeed. Being a mother can be such a humbling experience. Who needs one more potential knock to their self-esteem? That's where courage comes in. How many great dreams never get taken down out of the box on the shelf? It takes a lot of courage to take your dreams out of the box and hold them up in the light of day.

I have my own story of persistence. Remember the newsletter I worked on with my playgroup friend? It wasn't exactly what you would call a success. We didn't lose money, but we never really made money either. So after we stopped publishing, I put my writer's hat in a box on the shelf. A year or so later, I received a call from an organization that supports mothers of preschoolers, MOPS International, asking if I would be interested in writing for their newsletter. This was a big deal! Their newsletter was mailed to about ten thousand moms at that time. Once again my answer could have been yes or no, but "God's gifts and his call are irrevocable" (Romans 11:29). I persisted through my doubts and answered God's call by taking my writer's hat out of the box and dusting it off. Saying yes to this opportunity has led to me writing articles in magazines as well as books and more! Writing has become my passion—a new outlet for my creative self.

Are you still not sure what to do or how to start? Begin expanding your horizons by exposing yourself to as many new ideas and experiences as possible. If you aspire to be a writer, immerse yourself in literature. If you see potential in yourself as an artist, surround yourself with prints of paintings. If being a web designer sounds interesting, sign up for a class at the local community college. Provide yourself with as much raw material to work from as possible. The creative process of mixing and matching ideas and concepts can allow you to find your true passion.

"We have different gifts, according to the grace given us" (Romans 12:6). At a women's retreat I attended, a speaker talked about five general areas of giftedness we can find within ourselves. See if you recognize yourself in one or more of these descriptions:

Supporter—gives compassionate personal and emotional support to others

Hostess—provides a comfortable environment in her home and at other functions

Teacher—excels in compiling information and relating it to others in a format they can understand

Leader—a natural organizer and director

Encourager—lifts everyone's mood and makes others feel better about themselves

According to Arthur F. Miller, Jr., "The surest way to unlock the essence of a person is to look at what he or she likes to do and does well." Consider how the thing you are passionate about meshes with the areas of giftedness described above or with a more specific God-given gift. A good "fit" makes it easier to follow a dream, because the pursuit feels like fun instead of work. However, don't overlook the possibility that God may be nudging you to develop a latent talent (as with writing in my case).

Our brains were meant to handle more than feeding schedules and remembering which speed dial number on the phone is the pediatrician's. If it's been awhile since your mind has moved beyond the day-to-day, try some "stretching" exercises. Rediscover the child inside yourself who has yet to learn that some answers are "wrong"—who is not afraid to take a chance and make a mistake. A favorite tactic in brainstorming sessions is to consider all imaginable ideas about a subject. Nothing is too absurd or impractical to go on the list. Ideas build upon ideas. Refuse to accept that there is only one right answer to a question, and continue looking for more innovative solutions.

Let your mind wander after you have learned, read, or seen something new. Allow ideas and experiences to incubate. This method of free association is great for creative problem solving as well as for pointing you in new directions. Most people find the most fruitful time for these mental exercises is while you perform those mundane tasks that make up so much of the day: washing the dishes or laundry, cleaning house, taking a shower, or working in the garden. Just take a deep breath, relax your mind while your hands are busy, and let your creative ideas flow.

I once heard the definition of the word "crazy" quoted as "doing the same thing you've always done and expecting a different result." Children approach things with the attitude of an explorer—every experience has the potential to produce a new discovery. We can put this same way of looking at the world into practice by reading different kinds of books and magazines, talking to different kinds of people, and visiting different places. Use these additional mind expanders to help discover new interests or rediscover old ones:

- Try to read a different part of the newspaper each day, or subscribe to a weekly news magazine.

- Commit to trying out one new interest that engages your mind. Attend a free lecture at a local college or library to start.

- Listen to literary classics recorded on cassette tapes or CDs while you exercise. (Most libraries have a good selection of these to check out at no cost.)

One of the most difficult steps in following a dream in the beginning is just getting started. When I start a new writing project, I usually spend a period of time staring at an empty page. The enormity of the task overwhelms me—the number of choices seems limitless. It's only after I've written a couple of sentences that I even conceive, "Yes, I can do this." Another challenge that comes as you begin to realize some part of your dream is being able to "own" your accomplishment.

It wasn't until after my first book was published that I told people I was a writer when asked, "What do you do?" I had a hard time accepting that this was the Lord's plan for my life, that He gave me these abilities and everything else I needed to follow this new dream. God's gifts make our achievements possible. We deny Him when we do not own our accomplishments and give God the glory for them.

When God plants a passion in your heart, He places it there for a reason. It may take a year or a lifetime to pursue, but He will help you realize it. My mother-in-law gave me a bookmark a couple of years ago inscribed with this sentiment, "It is never too late to be what you might have been." God has given each of us the gifts to discover our dreams, chase them, and turn them into reality. All we have to do is make the time.

Mom's Moments

Ask a friend to be your accountability partner in pursuing a dream. The simple act of confiding your plans to someone can give you a nudge to get started. Ask your partner to provide encouragement on your journey toward realizing your dream.

Philippians 1:6 says, "He who began a good work in you will carry it on to completion until the day of Christ Jesus." Trust that God will help you find a way to pursue your passion, even when there seems to be no way.

Be intentional about noticing areas of giftedness in your child. Provide resources to help him or her cultivate their imagination and creativity.

Relaxing the Reins

When I was a child, I talked like a child,
I thought like a child, I reasoned like a child.
When I became a man, I put childish ways behind me.

1 CORINTHIANS 13:11

Even in this season, when our children are young and dependent for so much, they continually ask us to let go in some form or fashion. We can view childhood as one big transition or a never-ending series of smaller ones. For young children, most transitions require them to separate from something, starting with that first big physical separation from mom at birth. Regardless of how healthy a mom feels during pregnancy, most of us are ready for labor to start after the discomfort of that ninth month. Hence the exclamation many moms are said to make during delivery: "Get it out!"

How traumatic that entry into the world must be for newborns. The cold, the noise, the light—no wonder they cry as soon as they arrive! Moms, too, feel conflicted about the birth experience. We finally get to see who it is that we've endured heartburn and swollen ankles for, not to mention twenty-four hours of excruciating labor (a fact that we plan to hold over their heads for the rest of their lives). Moms also must contend with a physical recovery and hormonal changes that have us laughing one minute and crying the next (with more of the minutes being spent in the latter activity). Some moms must also deal with another immediate separation if their babies stay in the hospital for postpartum treatment. Both of our sons had to stay in the hospital after I was discharged in order to correct their unique medical conditions. In my experience, there are few things that feel as bad as having to leave the hospital without your baby in your arms. Once you and your baby are home, however, separation issues continue to crop up, one right after the other.

Child development experts say that strong, positive early attachments lay the foundation for later independence in kids. However, it's moms that may actually have more difficulty with being separated during this time. I myself was afflicted with what I call the "Mother Bear Syndrome." You know how mama bears are fiercely protective of their cubs? When I brought my first child home, I hardly wanted him out of my sight. Nobody could care for him the way I could—or so I thought. I jealously doled out the amount of time anyone could even hold him. My husband wisely indulged me and bided his time. As my son grew and being on call twenty-four hours a day took its toll on me, I began to relax. My earlier actions transformed until I almost wanted to say, "Take my child, please!"

A mother's angst surrounding early separation experiences often turns to exasperation as our children engage us in the perpetual tug-of-war over control. This battle marks life from the age of about six months until adulthood. Sometimes we pull away and our child resists. Sometimes our child pulls away and we resist. Back and forth, forth and back. Knowing when to relax the reins of control is not easy. One minute our children start to crawl away from us while smiling triumphantly over their shoulder, the next they cry uncontrollably when we leave the room.

There are stages in our children's development that we look forward to finishing, like the end of potty training and not having to help put on or tie their shoes. Doctors have put together general developmental timetables for when kids should pass this milestone or master that ability. Yet God endows our children with their own unique schedule for overcoming each developmental hurdle. Have you ever wished your child would hurry up and pass through a developmental stage before he is ready? When we try to rush either our child's or God's timing, the results can range from simply unexpected to decidedly unpleasant.

Our first two children were born nineteen months apart. We really didn't want to have two kids in cribs, so a month or so before my second due date we moved our son to a toddler bed. I think he would have been happy to stay in a crib, but he adjusted to the new sleeping arrangements well, with one exception. Almost every night during that month, my husband or I would be startled from sleep to find a pair of eyes peering at us from the side of the bed.

Surprise! Instead of going back to sleep when waking at night, as he did in the crib, our son got up to pay us a visit. He never said anything or even crawled into our bed, instead he just stood there and stared. I think it was more disquieting to be awakened by his staring than by a gentle shake! In any case, his nighttime prowls further disturbed my already restless sleep and tended to make us all crabby the next day. In this instance, we should have spent the extra money and invested in another crib.

When your child is four or five months old you may think you have this separation "thing" well in hand. You've played peekaboo enough times that your baby seems to know you will come back after a momentary disappearance. Your child shows no reluctance to staying in the church nursery. Then it hits: separation anxiety. I've heard that a child's response to separation may range from quiet acceptance to inconsolable crying. Unfortunately, I've only experienced the inconsolable crying response. Talk about heart-wrenching! It's not as if moms don't feel guilty and vulnerable enough about leaving their children in the hands of a capable caregiver to go to work or out to dinner. Our youngest son actually cried so hard one night when my husband and I were going out for a date that he threw up the dinner I had lovingly prepared and fed him ahead of time.

A friend of mine worked at a local "Mother's Day Out" program. She felt a special attachment to one little girl who missed her mother so much that she would periodically cry. The little girl touched her heart in more ways than one. My friend would think, *What a neat thing to have a child miss their mommy.* Her own independent girls were old enough she had to chase them down to say good-bye. She recalled asking her own daughters, "Can't I have a kiss before I go?" But her daughters would already be busy with something else. The girls' apparent indifference confused their mom—she expected a more dramatic response.

However your child responds to separation anxiety, here are five coping strategies you can try to make the time of separation less traumatic.

1. Give a clear explanation of where you and your child will be. Explain what you will both be doing while you are gone. In terms your child can understand, tell her when you will be returning. ("Mommy will be back after naptime.")

2. Make a relaxed visit to the new caregiver's place or to a new school. If you have a first-time baby-sitter coming in, invite her over on a day before you plan to be gone to learn the lay of the land and play with your child. One mom said she always invited new baby-sitters over on an afternoon simply to enjoy an

ice cream sundae with her kids—a great get-to-know-you visit!

3. When the time comes to separate, don't draw out your good-byes. Do be sure to tell your child you are leaving so as not to erode his trust by sneaking away.

4. Let your child keep a comforting "transitional object" from home with her whenever you are separated. If your child is really attached to a transitional object, pick up an extra one to keep in reserve in case the first is lost. We went through three versions of a certain stuffed dinosaur with one of my children.

5. Read books to your child that share what it is like to be apart and then reunited. Good examples are *The Runaway Bunny*, and *Are You My Mother?*

While separation anxiety may continue to appear in one form or another throughout the preschool years, children further confound us by simultaneously pulling away and asserting their own independence. One day they'll run around the corner at the end of the aisle in the grocery store and not come right back. Young children are famous for pulling their hands from their mother's grasp while walking in a busy parking lot. Their darting away leaves the mom to decide in a split second whether to run after the child or stop the shopping cart before it crashes into a brand new SUV.

The number of hugs and butterfly kisses you receive slowly declines. Our children pull away from us, often before we are ready. It can be difficult to know what our response should be. The Bible tells us that everything happens in its appointed time, a period which is not always under our control.

There is a time for everything,
and a season for every activity under heaven:
a time to be born and a time to die,
a time to plant and a time to uproot. . .
a time to embrace and a time to refrain.
   (Ecclesiastes 3:1–2, 5)

Often mothers must refrain from helping so a child can move past the next milestone on their own. As much as we want to rush in and spare our kids the frustration and pain of failure, encouraging them to persist when something is hard helps them become problem solvers. So we watch as our baby first bats at a toy, then reaches and misses, then carefully steers her hand to the toy and grabs it successfully. She builds upon the lessons of each failure to eventually succeed.

A toddler earns many of his accomplishments at a price to his person. Our youngest son never deemed it necessary to learn to crawl. At thirteen months he could stand and take tentative steps, but he never went far. One afternoon I was sitting on the floor, holding his hand to support him during "walking practice." All at once he dropped my hand and took off running. Unfortunately, his body started moving faster than his feet, and he hurtled around the corner of the room somewhat like a runaway locomotive. I was so shocked that I couldn't get to my own feet fast enough to help him avoid the collision with the wall in the next room. Instead, I heard the crash. I found him crumpled on the carpet with the beginnings of a black eye adding insult to injury. Ouch! He had earned his first battle scar in the separation tug-of-war. The wall won, and he took toddling a little more slowly for the next few days.

Why is it that we have such a hard time relaxing the reins of control over our children? As Carol Kuykendall writes in her book, *Loving and Letting Go*:

> *Letting go is confusing because it presents us with a conflict between head and heart. In our heads, we know our goals. We want to toughen, prepare, teach, and release our children. But sometimes our progress is thwarted by the instinctive, protective love in our hearts.*[12]

This instinctive heart love often overrides the knowledge that we cannot claim ownership of our children. "Sons are a heritage from the Lord, children a reward from him" (Psalm 127:3). Our children are God's sons and daughters, too; He has entrusted them to our care. By remembering that the Lord is sovereign over their lives, we can be confident that they still rest in His hands when we relinquish control.

Abraham demonstrated his faith and trust in the Lord's supremacy by obediently following God's command to sacrifice his son. Sarah, Abraham's wife, gave birth to her only child, Isaac, when she was well past her childbearing years, so he was truly a gift from God. How Abraham must have felt when the Lord told him to go to Mount Moriah, the place intended for Isaac's sacrifice! Abraham knew that God had only entrusted Isaac to him, not promised the child would be his forever. So instead of holding tighter to his son, Abraham surrendered him back to the Lord.

> *When they reached the place God had told him about,*
> *Abraham built an altar there and arranged the wood*
> *on it. He bound his son Isaac and laid him on the altar,*
> *on top of the wood. Then he reached out his hand and*
> *took the knife to slay his son. But the angel of the Lord*
> *called out to him. . . . "Do not lay a hand on the boy," he*
> *said. "Do not do anything to him. Now I know that you*
> *fear God, because you have not withheld from me your*
> *son, your only son." (Genesis 22:9–12)*

At this stage in our children's lives, we are not called to relax the reins in big ways—certainly nothing near God's request of Abraham. Instead, we are doing our part to lay the groundwork so that when those bigger issues confront us we can let go and give our children the freedom to make their own choices. The base of this foundation is built with the love and security we provide in the early years. We add another layer by developing trust and demonstrating confidence in our children as they take baby steps away from us. But in order for kids to make the right choices as they grow, we must also provide them with a godly foundation.

Mothers best help their children know the Lord when their own relationship with Him is strong and vital. We have so many reasons to praise God! Take time during the day to communicate your thanks for His love and your trust that He will continue to provide whatever your family needs. If you're not sure where to start, use this verse from the book of Psalms: "Let the morning bring me word of your unfailing love, for I have put my trust in you. Show me the way I should go, for to you I lift up my soul" (Psalm 143:8).

Over time our children will internalize the examples we provide through our behavior and attitudes. We must remember that, ultimately, we are raising our children to serve God, not to serve us. Seeing a mother who loves the Lord and follows the precepts set by Scripture helps kids sense that God is real. There are also specific things we can do to give our children a strong spiritual foundation based on their level of development.

Babies

Babies love to hear their mommy's voice. Pray out loud while you rock and cuddle your baby. You don't have to worry about saying the wrong thing. Just pour out your heart and mind to God. Sing songs like "Jesus Loves the Little Children." If you don't know many Bible songs, there are loads of tapes and CDs with children singing Christian music for you both to enjoy. When you play with your baby, ask him or her, "Who loves you?" Answer: "I do, and God loves you, too!"

Toddlers

Start a collection of board books with Bible stories. Your child will find these stories as interesting as any other, so read them often. Continue to pray with and over your child. Ask your child to help you finish a prayer. Introduce your child to the church nursery (stay with her if necessary) so that church becomes a safe and comfortable place for her. When you go on walks together, point out interesting things you see, and talk about how God made all things.

Preschoolers

Kids this age may be very interested in the story of Jesus dying on the cross, but they will likely not understand an abstract concept like salvation. Emphasize that Jesus is their friend. Preschoolers will ask a lot of questions, including many that we don't really have answers for. Give short, direct answers when you can, and when you can't, say "I'm not sure." Use teachable moments to point out God's care for your child as well as timeless biblical principles.

If your child has trouble remembering who to pray for at bedtime, teach her the "Hands-Up Prayer" technique.[13] The pointer finger reminds us to pray for people who point us in the right direction, like pastors and teachers. The middle finger is the tallest, so use that finger to remember to pray for "big" people in kids' lives like parents, grandparents, and caregivers. The ring finger is not very strong—it reminds us to pray for people who are less fortunate. The pinkie finger reminds kids to pray for the smaller members of God's family, themselves. By encouraging your preschooler to take an active role in prayer, you help him develop his own unique Christian identity.

In the early years of mothering, it's hard to look up from your child's seemingly endless list of needs and realize that your goal is to work yourself out of a job. Can it be that someday we will no longer be called upon to cut up someone else's food or kiss an injury to make it better? As our children become more independent, will they adhere to the wise man's saying of Proverbs 4:13? "Hold on to instruction, do not let it go; guard it well, for it is your life." Mothers must trust that the lessons our children have learned from us will be remembered and will serve them well in the next stage of their lives, and the next. Today they talk, think, and reason like children. It's only as we let kids go, baby step by baby step, that they move on to start putting childish ways behind them.

Mom's Moments

Dads are generally more willing to let kids adventure past what moms would consider the "safe" zone. Accept this as an important part of his role in their lives. If you're afraid to watch, go relax in the bathroom.

Have you released your child into God's care? If you are wrestling with control issues, either your child's or your own, remember that you can stand on the promise of God's faithfulness. "And we know that in all things God works for the good of those who love him, who have been called according to his purpose" (Romans 8:28).

Is the Lord sovereign over all areas of your life? "Unless the Lord builds the house, its builders labor in vain" (Psalm 127:1). Identify one area in your life where you have not relinquished control and present it to God in prayer.

Afterword

The first day I dropped my third child off at kindergarten, he marched into class so proud and excited, without any hesitation. He had spent years taking in the example of his two older siblings and was ready to go. Even though I felt a twinge, I was ready, too—in stark contrast to the day I dropped my oldest child off for his first day. I cried the whole way home. This time, as I walked down the hall, the school secretary offered me a tissue from the box she was carrying. On this day six years ago, I probably took two or three. It felt good to say, "No, thank you," even though finishing this chapter of my life was bittersweet. At least now I don't have to lock myself in the bathroom to have a few minutes alone!

Give thanks to the Lord, call on his name;
make known among the nations what
he has done.
Sing to him, sing praise to him;
tell of all his wonderful acts.
Glory in his holy name; let the hearts of those who seek the
Lord rejoice.
Look to the Lord and his strength;
seek his face always. (Psalm 105:1–4)

Notes

1. Dr. James Dobson, "Watch Your Words," Focus on the Family (June 2002): 11.

2. Dr. William Sears and Martha Sears R.N., "Solid Foods: When, What and How," *Baby Talk* (September 1992): 27.

3. Dr. Marianne Neifert, "No More Food Fights," *Parenting* (February 1996): 100, 102.

4. "Stats and Studies," *Children's Ministry* (July/August 2001): 11.

5. Crystal Bowman, "Books that Mothers Write," *MOMSense* (March/April 2003): 9.

6. Gary and Carrie Oliver, *Raising Sons and Loving It!* (Grand Rapids, MI: Zondervan, 2000), 49–50.

7. Dr. Henry Cloud and Dr. John Townsend, "Raising Great Kids," *MOMSense* (February/March 2001): 15.

8. Richard J. Foster, *Celebration of Discipline* (New York, NY: Harper San Francisco, 1998), 105-106.

9. Sharon A. Hersh, *Bravehearts* (Colorado Springs, CO: WaterBrook Press, 2000), 10–11.

10. Elisa Morgan and Carol Kuykendall, *Children Change a Marriage* (Grand Rapids, MI: Zondervan, 1999), 27.

11. Elisa Morgan and Carol Kuykendall, *What Every Mom Needs* (Grand Rapids, MI: Zondervan, 1995), 61.

12. Carol Kuykendall, *Loving and Letting Go* (Grand Rapids, MI: Zondervan, 1985), 32.

13. Alecia Glaize, "Hands-Up Prayer," *Exploring Faith* (Spring 2002, Vol. 2, No. 3, Leaflet 10): 8.

About the Author

Cynthia Sumner's gentle humor and practical insights speak to the needs of mothers today. She has been the contributing editor of the *MOMSense* magazine published by MOPS International for the past eight years and is the author of two books: *Time Out for Mom. . .Ahhh Moments,* and *Planes, Trains, and Automobiles. . .with Kids!* Cynthia is also a founding member of the MOPS Speakers' Bureau. She and her husband, John, live in rural Illinois with their three children, Spencer, Shelby, and Ross.

For information about speaking engagements, contact:

Speak Up Speaker Services
1614 Edison Shores Place
Port Huron, MI 48060
Phone: (888) 870-7719
E-mail: speakupinc@aol.com

Visit Cynthia's Web site at:
www.cynthiasumner.com